D1549870

Cameos of the Western Front

# Salient Points Four

Ypres Sector 1914 - 1918

By the same group of authors in The Cameos of the Western Front series*:

*The Anatomy of a Raid*
*Australians at Celtic Wood, October 9th, 1917*

*Salient Points One*
*Ypres Sector 1914 - 1918*

*Salient Points Two*
*Ypres Sector 1914 - 1918*

*Salient Points Three*
*Ypres Sector 1914 - 1918*

*A Walk Round Plugstreet*
*Ypres Sector 1914 - 1918*

*Poets & Pals of Picardy*
*A Weekend on the Somme with Mary Ellen Freeman*

*A Haven in Hell*
*Everyman's Club, Poperinghe*

*In the Shadow of Hell*
*Behind the lines at Poperinghe*

First Published in 2004 by
Leo Cooper/an imprint Pen & Sword Books Limited
47 Church Street
Barnsley
South Yorkshire S70 2AS

Front cover design by Ted Smith from an idea by Jim Ludden

A CIP catalogue record for this book is available
from the British Library

ISBN 0 85052 932 8

Typeset by IMCC Ltd. in 9.5 point ITC Bookman.
Printed in Great Britain by
CPI Bath.

# Cameos of the Western Front
# Salient Points Four
## Ypres Sector 1914 - 1918

by Tony Spagnoly and Ted Smith

with an introduction by
Ann Clayton

LEO COOPER

# CONTENTS

# DEDICATION

This book is dedicated
to the memory of
John (Jack) Edward Davis
1895 – 2003
and men of the 6th Battalion
Duke of Cornwall's Light Infantry

*"They were good fellows, this Service Battalion – officers and men."*

Page 132, The History of the Duke of Cornwalls Light Infantry 1914-1919
compiled by Everard Wyrall.

## ACKNOWLEDGMENTS

SPECIAL THANKS are always due to the Commonwealth War Graves Commission, and Public Record Office/National Archives for the cooperation and assistance of their staffs – and more so now with their respective approaches to the internet. Life is certainly easier for the researcher with the continual development of their web sites.

Gratitude is extended to Mary Ellen Freeman and Nick Fear – Mary for the 2nd-Lieutenants Keith Rae and Raymond Lodge contribution and Nick for his account on the late Jack (John) Davis, 6th DCLI, to whom this book is dedicated. Mary also contributed much to the Lieut.-Col. J. Maxwell and Jack Davis account, while Wilf Schofield deserves a medal for his help with a multitude of research projects.

Thanks to Alex Kallis of Oberstenfeld, Germany for his contribution in identifying German unit histories and maps and for providing detail on participants of the 126 Infanterie Regiment at Hooge on 30 July, of which his great grandfather, Josef Singer, was one. Thanks also to Keith Rae's family for their cooperation and contribution.

Gratitude is offered to Mrs Margaret Wilmington of New South Wales, Australia who gave permission to quote from her book, *Diaries of an Unsung Hero*, a tribute to her Uncle L/Cpl A. R. M. Stewart, who died of wounds at Ypres in 1917 with the 17th Battalion A.I.F. Likewise to Willy Mohan who assisted with the story of the McDonnell brothers from Dublin who fell together with the 2nd Battalion Royal Irish Fusiliers at the Second Battle of Ypres in 1915, and a sincere acknowledgement to Walter Kudlick from Massachusetts, USA for supplying Harvard University Records of American Merrill Wainwright who died at Passchendaele in 1917, his war lasting only three days.

We are deeply grateful to Mr Barry Woodroffe who gave unlimited access to information and documentation from his family's archives – a gesture which has brought to the fore invaluable intelligence regarding the German Army's first use of 'liquid fire' at Hooge in1915. This archive is currently being processed for its eventual destination as a recorded archive for public access.

The information featured in the Keith Rae cameo in this book, together with the aforementioned archive and recently researched detail of the German perspective of the attack, will form the basis for a volume currently being manuscripted by Mary Ellen Freeman, something to look forward to.

Last, but certainly not least, the inhabitants of Ypres and its surrounding villages deserve a vote of thanks. The patience they show to the hundreds of visitors, coach-loads and otherwise passing through their villages and often walking across their land, beggars belief. It makes you wonder why they put up with it, but they do!

Tony Spagnoly and Ted Smith. September 2004

# INTRODUCTION

I AM PROBABLY very unusual in knowing of no member of my own family who served in the Great War. A grandfather, being a cabinet maker and therefore in a 'reserved occupation', spent his war in aircraft construction, but that is as near as I can get. Nevertheless, how well I remember my first visit to the Ypres Salient in the spring of 1987. We had just suffered a close family bereavement and I felt I needed to get away for a short time. The Great War had captured my interest over a number of years, and by chance I noticed a small advertisement for a 'Battlefields Tour' which seemed to be just what was wanted. And so it proved to be. That first sight of the memorials, and endless lines of headstones, stays with me still.

But a large number of questions have also remained with me – why was that cemetery called that? Who decided that this particular action should be commemorated like this? Who was that individual? What exactly happened on this spot? And so on. *The Salient Points* series has answered many of my questions, and continues to do so. Ted Smith and Tony Spagnoly have done a great service to all of us – 'France & Flanders' enthusiasts – in researching, writing and collecting the cameos which make up these books.

And now we have *Salient Points Four.* Many of the cameos look at individuals, but not just the 'great and the good'; included are the memories of the simple private soldier whose life was changed for ever here, like Jack Davis of the Duke of Cornwall's Light Infantry who lived to the grand old age of 109 but who never forgot his wartime experiences and in particular, an amazing chance meeting with his brothers along the Menin Road.

Of course stories of young officers are to be found here – often their careers are easier to research than those of Other Ranks – middle and upper-class families generate more paperwork and look after it as a matter of course! (A great-uncle in my husband's family, a private in the South Lancashire Regiment, lies in a grave at Bard Cottage – but until I found the grave, members of the family, even his own sister, having no documentary evidence, were convinced that he was 'blown to pieces' and had no grave or memorial at all.) One junior officer featured in *Salient Points Four* is 2nd-Lieutenant Keith Rae of the Rifle Brigade, who typified so well the ex-public schoolboy-Oxbridge background enjoyed by so many of his contemporaries who found their lives interrupted by, and often ended on, the battlefields of the Salient. These cameos illustrate the friendships forged in the early exciting days of going to war, when it was certain to be 'all over by Christmas'; friendships tested by the severest of hardships, and the terrible personal losses endured by all who served here. Ted and Tony, and their fellow contributors, have walked these fields and woods which have become hallowed ground in the eyes of those who survived and those who try to keep memory green; areas like Hooge, along the Menin Road, where Keith Rae fell in July 1915, where the visitor on a sunny August day cannot help but be deeply affected by the sight of thousands of Michaelmas daisies in full bloom in Hooge Crater Cemetery.

The quiet 'back' areas of the Salient, so well known to the soldiers in their all-too-brief periods behind the lines between periods of trench duties, are featured in these cameos too: Elverdinghe, with its often-empty streets and its château where I once – probably illicitly – strayed one warm September, when horse-chestnut fruits popped out of their shells with sharp cracks and rained down on me like hailstones; or the village of Neuve Eglise near Messines where the military service of Lieutenant Charles Jagger, renowned for his many post-war sculptures on the theme of men at war, came to an early conclusion owing to the severe wounds he received in April 1918. What happened in places like these is described in detail, so that visitors armed with this, and the other *Salient Points* books, can return to the scene and explore the paths and byways for themselves.

I think that this is what all of us who study the war, at whatever level, want to do: we want to commemorate the courage and service bequeathed to us by those men and women more than 90 years ago, by visiting, as often as we can, the places where it happened. And readers who cannot go in person will find themselves transported in spirit to that long ago Salient, which survives only rarely now in the memories of veterans – whose numbers lessen almost daily so that soon none will remain. But we can keep the memory green, and pass the word to others. *Salient Points Four* will help to fulfil this aspiration for, as the poet John Macrae wrote:

> *to you from failing hands we throw*
> *The torch: be yours to hold it high.*

Ann Clayton. September 2004

TRIBUTE

On 7 June 1999 a ceremony took place at the Ploegsteert Memorial inaugurating the sounding of Last Post at 7 pm on the first Friday of every month.

Organised and implemented by the local community through its Comité du Memorial de Ploegsteert, the monthly ceremony was devised to show their gratitude to, and to honour the memory of, the many thousands of Allied troops who made the ultimate sacrifice during the Great War of 1914–1918.

## EDITOR'S NOTE

Hooge is a 'must visit' area for many, if not all, visitors to the Great War battlefields around Ypres. Hooge Crater, Hooge Château and its stables, Zouave and Sanctuary Woods, The Culvert and The Menin Road are names that appear frequently in accounts featured in many divisional, regimental and battalion histories.

Major differences today, as well as its cultivated as opposed to war-torn condition, are that the Hooge Crater and Zouave Wood are there no more (although their sites are easily identifiable), and the military cemetery south of the Menin Road and the museum north of it are! Another, allowing for domestic dwelling and agricultural fencing, is that Hooge Château was rebuilt on the site of its war-ruined stables.

Four Cameos in this book cover events at Hooge, two of them on 30 July 1915 – the day the Germans first used 'liquid fire' as a weapon against the British in an attack launched at 2.45 am. Casualties to battalions of the 41st Brigade, 14th (Light) Division were heavy and, although much has been written of the awful deaths it caused, its delivery at the Hooge Crater lasted only two minutes – a terrifyingly successful surprise factor screening an infantry attack on a small, strategically important position – but it was the enemy infantry and its supporting *minenwerfer* and artillery bombardment that caused the casualties, not the liquid fire.

In the early afternoon, 12 hours later, a counter-attack to retrieve the lost ground was a predictable disaster. A 45-minute pre-attack bombardment coupled with using the same sorely depleted battalions that suffered the morning attack, supported by battalions they had relieved the night before, themselves having spent the previous 10 days in the trenches, was bad enough – but the ground configuration guaranteed the attack's failure. Protests by senior officers in the line against it taking place were overruled by Divisional Command – and the resulting losses were horrendous. These, added to the morning attack's casualties, left the 41st Brigade able to muster only 720 men from its original 4000.

For today's visitor to draw his or her own conclusions as to whether or not the counter-attack should have taken place, adopt a German machine-gunner's-eye-view by standing inside Hooge Crater Cemetery at the top of one of the dividing paths between the headstones and look down its length to the bottom. Pretend it's a sunny afternoon and you're firing a machine-gun. Then, to get a British rifleman's-eye-view, walk to the bottom of the path and look back up to where you were standing. Pretend you're tired and hungry, holding a revolver or a rifle and about to run up the path to attack the machine-gunner. In both cases, imagine that the cemetery is not there.

Simplistic maybe, but seriously thought-provoking.

A German machine-gunner's-eye-view of the counter-attack. 2nd-Lieut. S. C. Woodroffe 8th RB and Lieut. G L. Talbot died while cutting through the British wire 20-30 yards beyond the enclosure hedge at the bottom of the cemetery. The trees lining the left of the cemetery follow the approximate route of the OLD BOND STREET communication trench.

A British rifleman's-eye-view of the German held trench system which began about a third of the path's length from the top. A & B Coy., 8th RB would have attacked to the right of this path with C Coy. attacking to the right of the cemetery itself – between the OLD BOND STREET and NEW BOND STREET communication trenches. The crest of the ridge itself, the Menin Road, housed the German machine-gun nests.

(See photograph on page 46 and map on page 44 of the Lambs to Slaughter cameo).

## Jack Davis, 6th Battalion Duke of Cornwall's Light Infantry

After giving the exhortation at the Menin Gate at Ypres in July 2002, Jack was asked what words he would like to offer on his wartime experience to present and future generations and, if anything were ever to be written about those experiences what he would want most of all to be included in any such writings?

To the first part of the question he said:

*"We were lucky: as a family we all came home safely. I sometimes wonder why, but I am a fatalist and so do not worry over it. There was nothing that marked us out as being special; the men I served with had just as much right to survive – we were all the same, the only difference being: we survived, they didn't*

*My feelings throughout my my life were more of a vow that I made them which will always be in my mind. It was a terrible, terrible price to pay.*

*When I speak those words\* it is a sacred duty I have to fulfil because it means so much to me, knowing so many of my comrades did not return. Although it is very emotional, it is something I cannot fail to do."*

\* The Exhortation.

To the second part of the question he said, simply:

*"What I would like to have put down is meeting my two brothers in the frontline trench on the Menin Road."*

**John (Jack) Edward Davis passed away on 20 July 2003**

*Destiny has more resources than the most imaginative composer of fiction.*
The Jessamy Bride, Frank Frankfort Moore.

# 1

## A FAMILY MAN
"Halt! Who Goes There?"
Jack Davis, 6th Battalion Duke of Cornwall's Light Infantry.

THE NAME JACK DAVIS seems far too diminutive for the man who answered to it. Quietly spoken, with a ready wit and feeling for life, his wisdom and wise counsel had been cultivated over his 108 years. He was a man who was proud of his family which extended to great, great grand children. In May 2003 he celebrated the date which would have been his 85th wedding anniversary. Jack was, above all, a family man with a passion. It was a lifelong passion, one which for the sake of the love of two brothers, was to put him in the shadow of the firing squad.

Prior to the Great War he was a general assistant at the Liberal Club in Whitehall, London. As a 19-year old in 1914, swept along on a tide of patriotic fervour, he joined Kitchener's Army with others from the club and was drafted into one of the finest regiments of the day, The Duke of Cornwall's Light Infantry. In training with the 9th Battalion, he was one of a happy band of 30 'Cornish Cockneys', a rare breed in those days. A transfer he engineered to its 6th Battalion accelerated his progress into war, taking him to the continent and into the desolation of the Ypres Salient, Belgium. With 'The Shiny Sixth', he experienced active army life with a rhythm to it – four days in the front line, four days in support, four in reserve and four more at rest. Jack

Jack Davis, 6th Battalion DCLI.

wrote home wherever he was, but it was easier at rest with its fewer distractions. His letters kept him in touch with home and his dearly loved family.

He had three brothers. 27-year old Jim, a regular in the Welch Regiment, was wounded during the retreat from Mons in the early months of the war and was invalided out to civilian life. The other two straddled Jack in age, but both looked up to him. Percy John and William Isaac had family nicknames, the former Bob, the latter

1

Bob Davis, 9th Battalion RB.

Bill Davis, 9th Battalion RB.

Bill.[1] With their highly regarded brother in the army they both wanted to join up. At the time both worked in the Junior Naval & Military Club in London and both tried to enlist. Jack was relieved to hear that they had both been rejected and would therefore stay safely at home. 22-year old Bob was rejected on medical grounds, needing urgent surgery for a varicose vein, whilst Bill at 17 and, at most, looking like a 12-year old, didn't even get past the recruiting sergeant.

Jack's desire to keep his brothers at home was partly based on his knowledge of his battalion's experience under fire in Zouave Wood on the night of 30–31 July. The heavy casualties from this demanded a replacement draft of which he was a member. Also, the battalion's experience on 12 August 1915 when men of its C and D Companies, in billets in the cloisters of St Martin's Cathedral, Ypres, were being buried alive during the bombardment of the town. Under continuous shelling, those of the battalion who were able to, including Jack, attempted to clear tons of rubble with their bare hands before a pioneer unit of the King's Liverpools took over the task.[2] The battalion's Maj. Bennett and Adj.-Lieut. Blagrove, both well known to Jack, were killed by shellfire and buried later at what was to become Ypres Reservoir Cemetery close to where they fell.[3]

Jack was an officer's servant and, from his work at the Liberal Club, he knew how a gentleman's comforts could be managed. Conditions of war presented no barrier to his efforts. His officers' cuisine was legendary, offering the palate a country-fresh, homemade feast, even if some of it had came out of tins. Complementing the ambiance of the table was the results of Jack's skills. He conjured up fresh fruit and flowers, non-military cutlery and clean table linen, and he was sought after to prepare officers quarters as the need arose.

When the actions at Hooge closed after the disaster of 30 July and the overwhelming success of the 9 August attack, there followed a period of comparative quiet for the 6th DCLI and the 14th Division as a whole. High command was preparing for an assault on the Loos–Givenchy line north of the La Bassée Canal on 25 September. Subsidiary operations at Pietre, Bois Grenier and

Bellewaarde would launch on the same date. The 3rd and 14th Divisions were to form the attack force at Bellewaarde with the 14th Division's front extending from Railway Wood to the Menin Road. Its 42nd Brigade would make the attack with the 5th King's Shropshire Light Infantry, 5th Oxfordshire & Buckinghamshire Light Infantry and the 9th Rifle Brigade. Jack's 6th Battalion DCLI, 43rd Brigade, were to act as reserve.

As the 25th drew nearer, Jack was detailed to finish his rest period early and go to the front line area at Hooge to prepare the dugouts for officers, signallers and reserve headquarters for the planned attack. He left a disintegrating Ypres by the Menin Gate and went forward, finding the communication trench full of water. He was forced from cover into a landscape of dank mud, rotting debris and water-filled shellholes. Jack scrambled through all this, slowly making his way forward, eventually re-entering the communication trench for a while before crossing the Menin Road, He then realised he was only a few yards from the forward area. Moving on into the line, his heavy feet and laboured progress attracted attention. He was challenged. 'Halt! who goes there?' Jack froze, not at the challenge, but at the voice:

The voice! It was so familiar. I thought: 'Wait a minute, I recognise that voice': it was that of my brother. When I looked – there he was. The standard reply to such a challenge is to give your name and number but no other information for the benefit of the Germans. Well! I gave myself away. I said 'Bob? It's Jack!" There, standing on the firestep of the front line out of the water in the trench, with waders up to their thighs, were my brothers, Bill looking through a periscope over the parapet. They had both been detailed for double guard duty and I had no idea that they had been able to join with me in the trenches and wanted to join me so that we could always be together. I'm not sure how they came out – whether devious or strings pulled – but they, like me, had been drafted as a result of the Liquid Fire casualties: perhaps fate had played a hand. Anyway, it resulted in that never-to-be-forgotten moment for me that saw us come together at Hooge as 'brothers-in-arms.

The fate that brought all three together still beggered belief in Jack decades after the event. Coming out of the pleasant shock of the meeting he found that his two brothers, somehow having overcome their unfit categories, had joined The Rifle Brigade. Jack felt that, somewhere along the line strings had been pulled. His brothers had wanted to join their soldier brother and had somehow managed to do so – and in a spectacular fashion. Bill and Bob had certainly worked at something together as the 9th Battalion Rifle Brigade's Nominal Roll of Other Ranks for the end of 1915 listed them with consecutive regimental numbers – S/12981 and S/12982 respectively. Jack wondered whether his Commanding Officer Col. Thomas Richard Stokoe DSO, a man with a reputation for his compassion, had been involved and, by detailing Jack to prepare dugouts at the front, had virtually assured the meeting would take place. It is quite possible that Rifle Brigade officers had passed information to DCLI officers regarding the Davis brothers' arrival in their ranks.

It would have been comparatively easy for them to set up the guard duty in the trenches and inform Col. Stokoe accordingly. Conjecture maybe, but it supports Jack's feeling that 'strings had been pulled'.

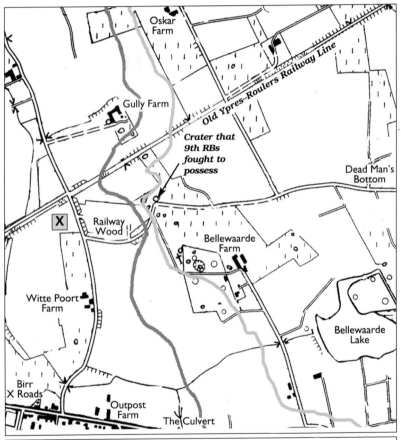

X marks the approximate spot where the Davis brothers met.
**Mid grey** line indicates British front line.
**Light grey** line indicates German front line.

The approximate spot today at Railway Wood, Hooge where Jack Davis met with his two brothers, both with the 9th Rifle Brigade in the front line just before the Second Attack on Bellewaarde in 1915.

Communications and socialising between the regimental officers of Kitchener's Army was always at a much higher level than that of the Regular Army. The same could be said with the relationship between officers and other ranks (although socialising would have been restricted by military regulations), particularly so in the 14th Division. Officers and men had often served together in Officer Training Corps at the same schools, universities or colleges and the relationships between brother officers and other ranks in the battalions, and between battalions, was of a totally different nature to that of their of the professional army counterparts.

Jack learned from his brothers that the family were in good health, home life, aeons away, was also well and fine. A long while of catching up was packed into a whispering moment of time, Bill imparting news while staring through his periscope, with Bob doing the same whilst resuming his guard. But duty called. Jack had to leave and get on with preparing dugouts. Then, for a few hours the three brothers faced the same fate, working the same section of the Ypres Salient within yards of each other.

On 25 September, the Second Attack on Bellewaarde opened. A heavy bombardment began at 3.50 am with the attack force leaving its trenches to dig in close up to the barrage – each battalion split into two columns with defined attack objectives. At 4.30 am the ground attack was launched. The results were mixed. The 3rd Division astride the Menin Road failed to advance because of uncut wire and heavy machine-gun activity. This caused the right column of the 4th Division's 5th KSLI to fail to advance also. Its left column reached its objective, as did the right column of the 5th Ox & Bucks, but the latter's left column was taken out by machine-gun fire, leaving a gap between it and the right column of the 9th RBs, Bob and Bill's battalion. From this gap the 9th came under a major bombing attack and faltered. Its left column though had swept all before it, passing its objectives only to find itself on a hillside exposed to machine-gun fire and shelling from Oskar Farm, an enemy strongpoint north of the railway. The attack developed from the gap, followed by a counter-attack from Dead Man's Bottom, a fortified wooded area to the 9th RBs front. Added to all this came the onset of trench mortar bombardment and the 9th's line was forced back to the crater, one of four caused by mines blown at the start of the attack, where they fought grimly on. On the rest of the front the attack petered out and, by 8.30 am, the battle weary troops were scrambling back into their jump-off trenches. The 9th RB carried on fighting for possession of the crater until 4 pm before being forced to do the same thing. It's relief that evening by the 10th Battalion Durham Light Infantry saw 4 officers and 140 other

Oskar Farm. In 1915 machine-gun fire and shelling from this strongpoint caused serious casualties to the 9th Rifle Brigade. The heavily fortified woodland of the strongpoint Dead Man's Bottom was not replanted after the war and nothing remains to identify its presence today.

A German's eye view of Railway Wood from the site of Dead Man's Bottom. German machine-gunners raked the ground in the forefront of the photo as men of the attacking 9th Rifle Brigade emerged from the wood. Enfilade fire to the 9th's left flank from Oskar Farm added to its heavy casualty list.

ranks of the battalion leave Railway Wood to trudge back to its forward camp. There it recuperated, took in drafts to replenish its ranks, retrained and, by 13 October, it was back in front line. Relieved on the 21st, the battalion entrained to Poperinghe from where it marched to rest billets at Houtkerque.

In the meantime Jack, with the 6th DCLI had moved from the Ramparts at Ypres to dugouts nearer the line, before relieving the 5th KSLI just before midnight of the 25th. Later the battalion moved into the GHQ line north of the Ypres–Roulers railway. Here they stayed until the last day of the month before moving into bivouacs near Vlamertinghe. Jack had heard that comforts, warm baths and clean clothes were to be on hand for him and his comrades, even clean beds with fresh linen were rumoured but, on arrival, the battalion found its billets occupied and had to take to the surrounding hop fields, under canvas, to seek shelter.

In the following weeks Jack could get no news of the well-being of Bill and Bob, the inter-battalion grapevine passing on information between friends or family serving in other battalions being hard to maintain in battle periods. He was aware that the 9th RB had taken heavy casualties and no amount of comforts, under

A peaceful Bellewaarde Farm. This German redoubt would have rained fire on the 9th Rifle Brigade as its right column troops passed to the north of the farm. A troops-eye-view of the farm would have been more or less the angle from which the photograph was taken.

Railway Wood in 1915 pretty much in the same condition as the Davis brothers would have seen it during their 'stay' there.

The site of the crater on the edge of Railway Wood today which the the 9th Battalion Rifle Brigade fought so hard to possess during the morning and afternoon of 25 Sept. 1915

canvas or otherwise, would help him relax without knowledge of his brothers. Not knowing their fate completely overtook his thoughts. He established the whereabouts of the 9th RB's rest camp at Houtkerque and decided to go and find them. He left camp without permission, on or around 18 October, walking 5 to 6 kilometres on a route avoiding all military areas and anywhere that the Military Police might be active. Travelling through the night, he found the remnants of various battalions at rest in a camp largely composed of bell tents. In one tent he came across men clustered around a table on which the post had arrived. There was a sadness in the air not normally associated with postal deliveries. On the table were several parcels and envelopes that would never reach their intended destination as the men to whom they were addressed were missing or dead. Many of the parcels were being opened and their contents shared. Jack was delighted to see Bill amongst the assembly. He was uninjured. Bob had been wounded, although safely in hospital and doing well. Jack had time enough for a cup of tea and to share a letter from home with Bill before assessing the trouble he was in. Dawn was breaking, he would miss roll call and be pronounced AWOL. Near to exhaustion, he left to return to Vlamertinghe to face the consequences. Bidding farewell to Bill, he made his way back, once again evading the potential challenges on the way. He then surrendered himself.

Numbed by his experiences, but aware of the seriousness of his situation, his only recollection while in custody was that his return journey had been quicker than the outward one. A sergeant visited him with his officer's counsel. Stern faces reinforced the problem he had caused himself, his battalion, and his regiment. His brothers may have survived recent battle, but Jack's continued existence was now in question. The enormity of his situation concerned him, but it had all been worth it. Whatever his fate, he took comfort in the knowledge that his brothers were alive.

On charge, Jack was marched to report before his commanding officer, Col. Thomas Richard Stokoe DSO, who listened attentively to his explanation. Jack told the truth and remembered that, 'He believed me'. Given the choice of a full court marshal as was his right, or taking his commanding officer's punishment, he plumped for the latter. 'I thanked him and said yes to his punishment'. Without a pause Col. Stokoe quietly ordered:

Three days pay stopped, dismissed.

Jack thanked him again and was marched out. Once in private his emotions overwhelmed him, he crumpled with relief and tried to recover by writing home, although he never completed his letter.

The Davis brothers' war moved on and the three miraculously

survived. Jack became a causality of the 1916 Battle of the Somme and went on to see active service in Ireland before returning to the continent. Bob and Bill became machine-gunners. Bob transferred to the Royal Flying Corps as an aerial rear machine-gunner. Bill tried to join him, but the RFC had ceased recruiting and he stayed with the Rifle Brigade. Now a corporal he was in charge of a machine-gun crew when he was injured and taken prisoner on the Somme in 1918. His life was saved by a German surgeon trepanning a head wound in pioneering surgery. He finished his war in a German hospital from where he was repatriated, suffering epilepsy for another 3 years. He spent 40 years in the Civil Service, living to the age of 95.

At this point, in his tale, Jack accelerated forward to June 2001 and the unveiling of Andy De Comyn's thought-provoking, *Shot at Dawn* Memorial at the National Memorial Arboretum, Alrewas in Staffordshire. Jack reflected that if he had missed his direction on his way back to camp or Col. Stokoe had not been such a compassionate man, he too could have been shot for desertion.

All those unfortunate boys were shot by their own, many just had breakdowns. I was very emotional, I could have been a name on one of the posts there. To me it was a very very, sad emotional day.[4]

The approximate area in a field which housed the trench where Jack Davis met his 'brothers-in-arms' alongside Railway Wood at Hooge. The photograph is facing north, with Railway Wood on the right and the old Ypres–Roulers railway line, now a road, beyond the crest of the slope. (See map on page 4).

Jack experienced another emotional day in November 2002 when he revisited the area at Hooge where he met his brothers over 87 years previously. His smiles illuminated the old battlefield and his memories generously flowed forth. He sat in thoughtful contemplation staring back to the past in silence, later commenting that:

It was rather difficult to control myself emotionally.

Jack was not alone, it was so for many others there.

At the time Jack, at 108 years, was the oldest man in Britain and most probably the last surviving member of 'The Shiny Sixth'. He served through the London blitz narrowly missing death when a parachute mine drifted to earth near to his Air Raid Warden post on top of the BBC building in Upper Regent Street. He worked in various occupations until past retirement age and enjoyed membership of the British Music Hall Society, the Concert Artists Association, the Civil Service Club, Surrey Cricket Club and the Punch Club. On his 100th birthday, to his absolute pride and delight, the latter invested him with honourary membership. At 108 years old he could still sing songs and tell jokes with the consummate skill of a music hall artist. Recently awarded the Légion d'Honneur by the French government he was proud to wear this with his 1914-15 Star, Allied Victory Medal and British War Medal, complemented by the Defence Medal for service in the Second World War. Above all, he was proud of the right to wear his old Duke of Cornwall's Light Infantry cap badge on his lapel.

Jack was a man truly for the record books, but overall with a passion, a family man.

Notes:

I. The name Jack was also a family nickname. Christened John Edward, he was careful to mention that his surname was spelt without an 'e', not therefore Davies. Being born on 10 March, St David's Day, many thought he must be a Welshman. A Cockney Cornish Welshman would be an epithet, worthy of Jack.

2. A German 17-inch gun, firing from Houthulst Forest ten miles away, had caused the casualties. It was also suspected that there had been a German observation post directing the fire from the main tower of the Cathedral.

3. Two officers and 18 other ranks of the 6th DCLI died on 12 August in the bombardment on the Cloisters. The remains of 40 soldiers of the 6th's B Company were discovered in the Cloth Hall cellars in Ypres square after the war, victims of the same bombardment. They were laid to final rest, but exactly where remains a mystery for the present. Jack had made many visits to Ypres and attended the Menin Gate ceremonies, giving the exhortation at several of them. He regarded these pilgrimages as a sacred duty to remember the men, his friends, who fell on that day.

4. Jack was once detailed to form part of an execution squad. He reached the point where weapons were collected to find that, being last in the line, there was no rifle for him. He was spared a haunting duty and was, "very, very relieved".

*The night was about to turn into a glorious summer's day. In the park birds were twittering; light mist covered all traces of war. Now and again a gunshot, otherwise a Sunday-like quiet.*
*By 4 am it will be over.*
2nd-Lieutenant Wollinsky, 6 Kompagnie, 126 Infanterie Regiment

## 2
## FAITHFUL SOLDIER AND SERVANT
2nd-Lieutenant Keith Rae
8th (Service) Battalion
The Rifle Brigade (The Prince Consort's Own).

IN THE EARLY HOURS of the morning of 20 May, 1915, the 14th (Light) Division of Kitchener's New Army disembarked at Boulogne. One of its brigades, the 41st, was composed mainly of prestigious rifle regiments whose officers had been selected from Oxford and Cambridge Officer Training Corps: the elite of university and public school life. Many were friends from their school and university days, all with a relatively common background. However, amongst them was Thomas Keith Hedley Rae, ex-Balliol College, Oxford, who, although a Master at Marlborough College before his commission, had by-passed a public school education.

As a child Keith's weak eyesight and less than robust constitution, like his brother, Bino, prompted his father not to send the two to public school, unlike the two elder brothers, Charles and Leathart. Edward Rae's distinctive personality made its mark on the formation of the characters of his sons but none more so than with Keith whose sense of fun, duty and desire to serve others combined to produce a compassionate humanitarian with a spiritual love of life and people. Family life was central to Keith's upbringing where friends were warmly accepted into the fold. When a young man friends from Oxford were invited to spend holidays at the family homes in Birkenhead in winter and Rhoscolyn, Anglesey, in summer.[1] The family tradition, instigated by Edward, dictated that, on arrival, all guests were received in the dining room to compose prose or verse which was then collated in volumes that adorned the sitting-room table.

The most formative years of Keith's life began in 1907 at Balliol College. Shy and unassertive at first, he quickly found his feet, gaining confidence and charming others with a magnetic intensity and individuality. His friend, Ernest Crosse, from Balliol and Marlborough, said:

> Had Keith been to a public school, he would undoubtedly have derived some advantages from it, but it is hardly likely that his individuality and humanity would have been so marked.

The decision to choose Balliol was a fortunate one. The least hide-bound by convention of all universities, it brought Keith into contact with a group whose social consciences had an enormous influence on him. The religious life of the college ran under the guidance of the chaplain, Neville Talbot: a striking individual and committee representative for the Senior Common Room on a project set up for under-privileged boys in St. Ebbes, Oxford. After a Sunday morning meeting where a Labour MP addressed the young scholars on social issues, challenging them that living on intellect and leisure alone rendered them only 'alf-educated', Keith felt moved to offer his service to the boys club at St. Ebbes. Within a short time not only was he spending most of his evenings at the club, he also became the enthusiastic drive and momentum at the very heart of it. He was interested in the individual and believed that the key to this work was not so much establishing discipline as encouraging self-discipline. He influenced the range of activities available, even those he was more enthusiastic than skilled at, such as sport, where his friend, Ronnie Poulton, took the lead, having come up from Rugby School to Balliol in 1908, a year after Keith. Whilst at Rugby Ronnie had been involved in The Rugby Mission, also a project for under-privileged boys, and it was with instinctive familiarity that he began working at St. Ebbes with Keith. Few boys could have experienced the thrill of being coached by so gifted a player as Ronnie who would proceed to captain his country. Keith's personal forte were activities such as drama and music where he utilised his considerable talent as a pianist, though perhaps in a less formal manner than his skill could have permitted. Ernest Crosse, fellow-scholar and close friend, remembers Keith:

A Thames backwater at Oxford with Keith Rae (second from left) with his brother Bino (left), Ronald Poulton (second from right) and Billy Collier (right).

sitting at that old gimcrack piano thumping out Alexander's Ragtime Band until everyone was carried off their feet.

The most intimate circle of Keith's friends were drawn from fellow Balliol men involved with the work of the Club: men like Stephen Reiss who had come up to Balliol from Marlborough College in 1907. Reiss was deeply religious and very conscious of social issues and problems he felt needed to be addressed. The two scholars gravitated towards each other as kindred spirits and held a shared vision of the potential of the Boys Club. They set up education classes encompassing political debate, encouraging the boys to develop and express their own views, as evident in a letter from one of them to Keith:

Before I finish I shall be able to tie Mr. Bonar Law or F. E. Smith [others, including yourself] into knots about the management of our Empire. I am looking forward to the time when we shall be able to hold a debate between ourselves about the former, in which time I hope to be able to 'set on your ideas!'

This letter appears to confirm Keith's belief that every individual has an important contribution to offer if given opportunity and encouragement, a belief which was not only an intellectual idea but actively practised as a working philosophy. He encouraged equal participation of boys and men together, each learning from the other to produce a collective contribution of the group as a unit. Where individuals had to be in charge, they were to lead by example, a principle to which Keith attached the greatest importance and one upon which the foundation of his service as an officer in the Rifle Brigade would be laid. Although this tightly-knit group of friends were the core of the club, all volunteers, such as Poulton's friend Henry Bowlby, were embraced within its fold. Using his persuasive powers, Keith enlisted the services of countless fellow-scholars. Arthur Adam recalls:

You could no more avoid doing what he really wanted than you could walk into a German trench in broad daylight.[2]

It was the spiritual guidance of the boys that mattered to Keith and after four years - the last two as President - it was leaving the club he felt most when the time came to depart Oxford. Understanding that in spiritual terms he had received more than he had given, he wrote:

The life of service is not only the best, but the happiest as well.

In 1912 Keith moved to Marlborough College as an assistant. He had long hesitated between a career of social work in south London and a professional calling at the Bar. He gave fleeting consideration to ordination as a priest but, in his eyes, a black coat and dog-collar created a barrier where none should exist. His decision in favour of becoming a schoolmaster was reached by a process of elimination, and in deference to his father's wishes. Having only secondhand knowledge of public schools he saw them as vast machines bound by convention with little scope for individuality: qualities of the utmost importance to him. After a shaky beginning, especially in the realms of Greek and mathematics, where he had to teach himself in order to teach the boys, he found that the inner qualities he had discovered at St. Ebbes began to be unconsciously transferred to his pupils. Not only did he discover an aptitude for the job, but, remarkably for the times, he taught on an individual basis, even in the largest classes. To him, each boy was a separate being to be approached on a one-to-one basis. As the boys' respect for him grew, he was able to display his sense of humour and love of practical jokes, further increasing his popularity. At the same time his spiritual and philosophical outlook on life drew to him like-minded souls in the Common Room where he made friends with, amongst others, Freeman Atkey, Percy Wace and Ronald Gurner.[3]

When a position in Upper School became vacant, The Master, the Rev. St. J. B. Wynne-Wilson, offered Keith the post on condition he spend a term in Germany learning direct teaching methods. He readily accepted and spent the summer of 1913 at the Institut Tilly in Berlin. He returned to England on his beloved motorbike, 'Rudolph', taking a route through several countries, staying with Ernest Crosse and Henry Bowlby before arriving home in late July. His last year at Marlborough was a happy one. He was now a lieutenant in the Officer Training Corps where, at a 'brew' in 1914, he was asked by Maj. A. H. Wall to propose the customary health of the NCOs in front of the entire school and, above all, to 'make them laugh!' Initially daunted by the task, he eventually composed a funny ode about them. It brought the house down. That summer of 1914 saw friends from Oxford in abundance prompting a need for Rudolph's sidecar, with many late-night returns from Oxford, but such times would not last!

When war came Keith was in OTC camp at Tidworth, Wiltshire. He volunteered immediately as interpreter or despatch rider. Autumn

passed and he still found himself waiting. Thinking of how he might best use his time for others, he held classes of instruction for prospective officers amongst the boys. In December, the call came. Maj. Wall arranged for him to be gazetted to the Rifle Brigade under Ronnie Maclachlan, the only man, Keith used to say, who could talk him to a standstill. On 14 December 1914, he took his commission as 2nd-Lieut. in the 8th Battalion. So began his

Lt.-Col Ronnie Maclachlan, under whom Keith served.

Keith as a 2nd-Lieut. in the 8th Rifle Brigade.

Henry Bowlby, a friend from Keith's Oxford days.

2nd-Lieut. The Hon. G. W. (Billy) Grenfell.

most intense, if sadly brief, pathway to service. He was 25-years old.

Keith was delighted to find many Oxonians in the battalion such as Henry Bowlby, and also Billy Grenfell: someone he had not seen eye-to-eye with at Balliol.[5] Now the focus of his service was the men of 10 Platoon, C Company and he soon felt enormous sympathy for those older men who had "given up home, family and well-paid jobs" to enlist in Kitchener's Army. Ever anxious to embark for the front Keith summarised his feeling at a dinner with Ronnie Poulton and Ernest Crosse as '... better to be in the dentist's chair than in the waiting room.' In spite of the demands of training, many officers were able to enjoy social breaks from their routine. Ex-Marlborough College officers in the bat-talion such as Keith, Leslie Woodroffe and his youngest brother Sidney, organised what was described by Leslie as 'an amusing little Marlburian dinner' held on 18 April whilst at Rushmoor Camp. Marlburian friends from other regiments had been invited such as Capt. Tom Bourdillon, 8th King's Royal Rifle Corps, Capt. Percy Wace, and Lieut. Stephen Reiss both of the 5th Royal Berkshire Regiment. Lieut. 'Curly' Butterworth, 9th Rifle Brigade, and the much-loved master, Capt. John Bussell, 7th Royal Sussex, were prevented from attending at the last minute. Of this little gathering not a single invited member remained alive at the end of the war. Six days later on 24 April, the 7th and 8th battalions were inspected in the grounds of

Capt. Leslie Woodroffe.

2nd-Lieut. Sidney Woodroffe.

2nd-Lieut. Ronald Poulton.

Farnham Castle by Gen. Neville Lyttelton; the mood was then one of anticipation of the departure for active service.[6]

A month later orders to prepare for France were confirmed. Keith spent his last evening in England having dinner with his father and Ernest at a hotel in Aldershot. It was a reflective evening, all three men with mixed emotions having had news of Ronnie Poulton's recent death in action. The evening ended in the saying of goodbyes in the street outside with 'memories surging around us'. It would be the last time his father and his friend would see Keith alive.

The Division landed in France and spent its first days travelling on troop trains. Keith was concerned to see that the officers travelled first-class, whilst the men travelled in cattle trucks designed to: 'hold two cows comfortably but was requisitioned to hold 44 men!' Jokes from his days travelling on the local railway like: 'Passengers are requested not to alight and pick flowers while the train is in motion!' were shared amongst his platoon and he soon discovered a new-found confidence in handling men as opposed to boys.

On 7 June, the battalion saw its first action at Dickebusch. During its second day there an incident took place which greatly affected Keith and inspired his future conduct as both officer and man. During a voluntary tour of the wire in front of the trenches, fellow

Marlburian and platoon officer, Lieut. Albert Hooker, was wounded in the shoulder.[7] It was a wet night and Keith was distressed at the thought of his ex-pupil's one-and-a-half hour walk down muddy trenches to the dressing station. He had been asleep when Hooker was hit and on arriving at the scene was upset at witnessing the ordeal suffered by the wounded in such circumstances. His compassion roused, he wrote:

Keith's friend and ex-pupil Lieut. Albert Hooker.

Many people at home wrongly think that, once wounded, the worst is over. In many cases it takes an hour and a half to get a man down a wet communication-trench on a stretcher by night; by day it is nearly always impossible to move him at all. It is quite on the cards that a wounded man might have to be left 24 hours, merely bandaged up by a stretcher-bearer whose anatomical knowledge is not of the profoundest. And even if hit at night, the actual journey, bumped down a narrow trench in the dark, is a very terrible ordeal.

Having been received into the trenches by a Staff Officer who had commented: 'A very quiet night, nothing doing', Keith reflected:

I learnt what Oxford philosophers believe impossible - that Nothing is a relative term.

A week later the battalion was ordered to support a 9th Brigade attack at Hooge. The mood was tense as it waited, 'booted and spurred' as Keith called it, but, in the event, it was not needed.

During this wait he experienced the first death in the platoon when Rifleman John Cooper was killed by shell concussion whilst asleep.[8] The burial was a simple dignified ceremony:

> Three volunteers dug the grave and the body, wrapped in green tarpaulin, was lowered by them into it. Our chaplain read a few simple touching prayers by the light of his torch lamp. There was just the little circle round the grave in the middle of the green wheat field; we all bared our heads as the chaplain read the service; all men took a last look at their dead friend and the earth was heaped in.

The battalion retired for 10-days rest camp near Vlamertinghe, giving Keith the opportunity to visit Ypres, whose "utter desolation" left him struggling for adequate words of expression:

> It almost makes one doubt whether Man is higher or even as high as the animals.

On 29 June orders were received to take over trenches near Hooge. These 10 days were to prove the most intense of Keith's life. The platoon was to occupy support positions and act as ration-carriers to the front near Railway Wood. In the second line, 50 yards in front of Keith was another of his ex-pupils: 19-year old 2nd-Lieut. Sidney Woodroffe, who described this sector as "bestial". Keith's platoon

'C' Company officers relaxing at Rozenhill, Belgium, with Keith Rae (right) sitting alongside Lieut. Albert Hooker. To the left of Hooker are Company C.O. Capt. Foss Prior and fellow platoon officer Lieut. Boughey and bombing officer Capt. B. Pawle. This photograph was taken two days before Lieut. Hooker was wounded.

19

occupied a row of 14 'half-sunken, wholly verminous dug-outs' with a connecting trench only 2'6" deep, and the entire position under intense bombardment.

Three days later the battalion lost its first officer as Keith's platoon was delivering rations to A Company, in the second line. Two men of the platoon had been wounded on the way and A Company C.O. Capt. C. Balleine, had offered to see them evacuated to the nearby dressing station. After talking at length with the captain, Keith was moving his remaining men along the line when a deluge of gas shells came over and Balleine set about moving his troops further along the trench. A

shell hit the parapet and a sliver literally removed Balleine's head from his shoulders. Sidney Woodroffe, still recovering from a recent foot injury, put what was left of his captain's body onto a stretcher and helped carry it down to the dressing station on the Menin Road. On returning, he discovered that of the casualties in 4 Platoon during his absence, one corporal was still alive, though badly wounded. He doubled back to the

Capt. C. Balleine.

dressing station with a party of men in an attempt to save his corporal. They had a narrow escape when a shell exploded just 10 yards in front of them. Sadly, Corporal Duncan died of his wounds en route.[9] Keith felt that 'Providence' had taken a hand in sparing his platoon's involvement in the incident:

At best we should have been badly gassed, and at the most ...

2nd-Lieut. Sidney Woodroffe in trenches at Railway Wood. with fellow officers Scrimgeour to his right and Lieut. Gladstone and Capt. Sheepshanks to his left.

As a result of this shelling, Col. Maclachlan moved A Company from the line as the bombardment moved to concentrate on the corner of the road that ran past Keith's platoon dugouts.

These nightly carrying parties became hazardous exercises, the enemy shelling their every move. One of Keith's men, Rifleman Britland, describes the ordeal:

> We used to leave our trench about 9 pm and for the next 3 or 4 hours it was a case of 'Shells and how to dodge them'. The officer would come down the trench calling us out of our dug-outs. We would then leave the trench one at a time at intervals of 10 yards and run for all we were worth for about 200 yards ... When we got the rations, we had to carry them to our battalion HQ just behind the firing line ... One night we had to go almost bent double, carrying biscuits in large tin boxes. You talk about sweating - it simply poured off us ... When we got back to our trench, we would all breathe a sigh of relief and thank God that we had got back safely again.

The shellfire was prolific. On one day alone, Britland counted an average of between 200 and 300 shells bursting within a 300 yard radius. There was daily gas shelling under which, time and again Keith and his men went out to assist casualties from other units. Characteristically, Keith gives full credit to his men for their bravery. On their last evening in the line, an incident occurred which was to Keith as 'Paul's Revelation on the road to Damascus'. At 8 pm on 8 July a shell killed a nearby Royal Engineer and wounded another. An excited 'telephone fellow' ran into Keith's dug-out to ask for help. Keith ran out with his bugler, Rifleman Blake, to find the wounded engineer being tended by a sergeant of the machine-gun section. Under continuous shellfire, it took Keith and the sergeant 30 minutes to dress the wounds before a Rifleman Bell arrived with a stretcher. Keith and the sergeant then began their journey to the dressing station negotiating a full 150 yards before finding a trundle cart on which to place the stretcher. Then the sergeant received a bad facial shrapnel wound. Griffiths, another rifleman from Keith's platoon, took over the trundle cart leaving Keith and Riflemen Bell supporting the sergeant to follow him to the dressing station. The impact of this experience is evident in one of Keith's last letters to Ernest a week later:

> What is so inspiring is the spirit you see among the men and especially among the wounded. When we meet, as in God's mercy we will, I shall try and tell you of a half-hour I had with two wounded men and some of my priceless boys under a rain of shells. I cannot express what I mean, but it was the happiest moment of my life. We were all just on the brink of the Next World. Suddenly everything seemed to become clear, and one no longer 'saw through a glass darkly'; one felt certain

about what one had hardly previously understood at all. And fear and nerves and egoism all just vanished in the joy of just being there. I am not mad, and I will one day try and explain to you.

This 10-day experience was followed by a 10-day rest giving him time to reflect on so significant a turning point in his life. He felt he had found his rightful place in the world: a place from which his true self could be revealed. In a letter of 23 July he wrote:

Shells and bullets lift the veil which shrouds the real man from the apparent.

As news of casualties amongst ex-pupils, friends and Balliol men began to flood in, another letter to Ernest reveals his focus on the personal loss suffered by the death of Ronnie Poulton:

Nothing can come as a surprise since Ronald has gone.

After his recent experience, that of friends under fire began to occupy his thoughts and letters. He asked his father to contact Poulton's father for the grave location so that he might make a pilgrimage there. A letter to Mr Poulton reflects that even in the midst of his responsibilities he intended to honour his promise:

Many thanks for your letter. I was very anxious to go to Ronald's grave if I could, and leave a few flowers there. But it does not seem at the moment possible. I cannot say where I am, but I am many miles away at a very notorious and unpleasant spot. You know I will take any chance I have of getting there, and will let you or Mrs Poulton know the moment I have done so.

I cannot realize yet that Ronald has gone and I do not attempt to do so. For I firmly believe that Death is at most a temporary parting and that we may meet those we love after the grave...

The battalion prepared to return to Hooge to relieve the 7th Battalion which had held the line for the previous 10 days. The wisdom of using an inexperienced battalion in this part of the line is questionable. Maj. Billy Congreve's diary entry of 22 July notes:

It is a very wet evening and the 8th Brigade are being relieved by the 14th Division. I can't help feeling anxious at their being put into such a vile place as Hooge, especially in its present state. We have asked if we may stay on a week to put things right, but it has not been allowed.

Congreve's misgivings would prove well-founded. As the time of the relief drew closer, an amount of circumspection took place within the battalion. Sidney Woodroffe had already written to a friend:

There is going to be the hell of a battle soon. I bet you anything you like. The Germans I believe have massed about a million men and guns opposite this part, so we are led to believe.

With such speculation circulating, and in light of their recent experience of Hooge, the mood amongst many took on a more measured apprehension as reflected in a letter from Keith to Billy Collier:

Perhaps one day we may see something more of one another again as in the good old Oxford days. I wonder if you often look back, as I do, and wonder at the extraordinary happiness of those times? How seldom anything but tiny clouds passed our skies.

On 29 July, two days after this letter, the battalion moved into the line. After the war, fellow officer, Lieut. Gordon Carey wrote:

I remember having a strong presentiment as I plodded up the line that night that I should never come back alive. In the event I was the only officer to survive.

As the 7th Battalion trudged back to Vlamertinghe, the 8th began familiarising itself with its trenches centred around a large mine

Lieut. Gordon Carey.

crater. A Company took over Trench G10 to the left of the crater while two platoons of C Company, including Keith's, occupied Trench G5 to the right of it.[10] Shelling had rendered the crater unoccupiable, with contact between G5 and G10 possible only through patrolling. The 8th Battalion War Diary noted this factor as 'a positive invitation to disaster.'

As the battalion settled in, something struck the men as odd: there was no 'enemy hate' of any kind: no shells, no hand grenades or fire of any description: the enemy's routine practice on change-overs.[11] Several bombers tried to chivvy the Germans into response by lobbing hand-grenades over towards them, but to no avail.

At 3.00 am the trench garrison stood-to-arms in the grey light of approaching dawn. Massed in the enemy front line trenches and four purpose-built saps opposite were five assault companies of the 126 Infanterie Regiment awaiting an imminent signal to attack the unsuspecting riflemen. The objective of the enemy plan was to seize and secure all British positions across the high ground to within 200 yards of Zouave Wood. At 3.22 am the signal was given when a mine near the Hooge Château stables was blown. Suddenly, out of complete silence a fearsome united enemy barrage of machine-guns, artillery and *minenwerfer* opened up all along the British front lines; the vanguard of this attack being the deployment of flammenwerfer. Arcing the flames up to 30 yards to drop on the British position in order to pin down the garrison, the German assault force flooded rapidly across the short distance within minutes.

2nd-Lieut. Wollinsky[12], a young platoon leader in 6 Kompagnie, the eastern most flank of the German attack directly opposite Keith's section of Trench G5, describes the moment:-

... a muffled bang, a bright streak in the dark sky, an earsplitting noise and suddenly the sky is aflame, the earth burns & thunders. Artillery, mines & flammenwerfer spew their deadly fire into the

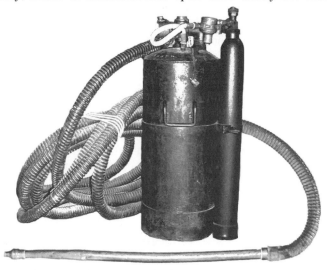

A flammenwerfer canister of the type used by the Germans in the attack on 30 July 1915.

The method of delivery – German troops under training in the use of the flammenwerfer.

enemy trench. Shadowy forms break from the German line, becoming more & more as those at the back seek to push through. In all, the one urge: to run forwards at the enemy, taking full advantage of surprise.

The two minute duration of liquid fire from seven large stationary canisters sunk into the ground by the crater provided a perfect screen behind which the German assault force moved rapidly and uncontested. The element of surprise was a masterstroke of invention and planning, providing a brief but crucial window of virtual British paralysis that gave maximum advantage to the attackers.

At the farthest point in his line from the crater, Lieut. Carey looked back across a lurid red sky capped by thick, black incandescent smoke, all accompanied by a sinister hissing sound. He saw three or four distinct jets of flame and for some seconds was stupefied, but as reason began to return his thoughts portray his horror at the unfolding scene:

... this is the end of the world, the Day of Judgement has arrived.

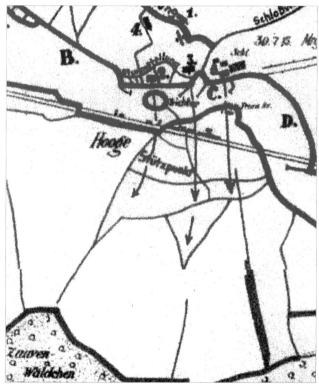

The German infantry attack screened by liquid fire. Map from 'Infanterie Regiment 126 in the World War'.

25

He then witnessed the first German wave gaining its foothold near the crater in Trench G5. This was garrisoned by Lieut. Milsom of No. 9 Platoon, with a small bombing party led by Bombing Officer Capt. Pawle at the crater itself.

Giving the defenders full credit later in their official history, the Germans, to their surprise, found a virtually intact garrison awaiting them. Using common sense the defenders had shielded themselves at the bottom of the trench in an instinctive attempt to avoid the flames. They rapidly reassembled themselves to greet their oncoming attackers who outnumbered them approximately five to one.

*(Contrary to popular misconception there were few direct casualties from flammenwerfer. 44th Field Ambulance and No. 10 C.C.S. Remi Sidings were visited on the following day, 31 July, to ascertain the extent of burns casualties and none were found, save two minor cases. The only casualty stated as burnt was the body of 2nd-Lieut. Milsom when found, although whether by flammenwerfer or explosive cannot be known. The enemy report stating that the British 'covered themselves' corroborates information such as that from Rifleman Fairhurst, C Company, who wrote from a P.O.W. Camp in October stating that most of the company had been killed by enemy bombers).*

2nd-Lieut. Wollinsky resumes:-

Enemy machine-guns are already clattering. Shrapnel bursts over the head of the stormtroops. A heavy mine whizzes away over them: an earsplitting noise. However, everything is nearly within reach. In one leap we are through the enemy defences. Now into the trench. In position against us are the 8th Bn Rifle Brigade, the first men of Kitchener's Army: young, strong, honourable people, but they cannot withstand the German impact. Almost immediately the first trench is cleared by hand grenades and the bayonet.

Carrying buckets of hand-grenades, advanced bombers in the initial German wave set about clearing the front line, with following waves 'mopping up' any continued resistance.

Keith's company commander, Capt. Foss Prior, had just returned from inspecting his men in G5 when the attack started. He was only seconds later than Carey in witnessing events, having telephoned an immediate 'Mines S.O.S.' to Battalion H.Q. from his position at the junction with Trench G3.[13] On looking behind him, the scale of the attack around the crater alerted him to the gravity of the situation facing his men who were directly in the path of the enemy advance:

They massed projectors at Z [fifteen yards from the edge of the crater] and then flamed them along our trenches left and right [flames mostly a screen] then poured men through on left and right of crater, where

Capt. Foss Prior

we were only allowed to put bombers. They came through in large numbers and I could see nothing of Nos 9 & 10 Platoons .. only about 4 are anything but missing : it must have been hand to hand there. The effect of the liquid fire was too horrible for words in its unexpectedness, combined with the shelling but I don't think it burnt much. It was really a splendid screen, but I shall never forget that moment.

On realising that his front line troops were overwhelmed by the enemy, he ordered the

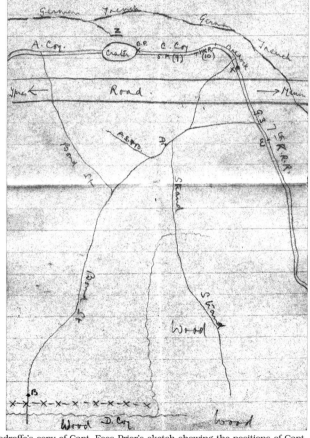

Leslie Woodroffe's copy of Capt. Foss Prior's sketch showing the positions of Capt. Bertram Pawle's bombing party (**B.P.**) adjoining the crater, Lieut. Sidney Milsom's No. 9 Platoon (**S.M.** [9]) east of the bombers and Keith Rae's No. 10 Platoon (**T.H.K.R.** [10]) at the bend of the trench as it curved to the Menin Road. **Z** marks the trench behind the crater from where the flammenwerfer were sited and **X** marks the site of Prior's headquarters

The resulting effect of British troops being trained in the use of 'liquid fire'.

remnants of his company to retire to the support positions.[14] With so few survivors, no clear picture emerged as to the fate of its defenders. Of the few who managed to reach Zouave Wood, Rifleman Griffiths was able to recount what he had last seen of his Lieutenant in the attack. This was recorded on 16 August aboard a hospital ship where Griffiths stated that:

> The last I saw of Lieutenant Rae was firing his revolver over the parapet of the firing trench.

Although he had seen him 'struck and he fell' he added, 'I feel almost sure that he was killed outright.', but Keith was simply reported as 'missing'.[15]

One of only six surviving riflemen, Harry Rogers was only 10 yards away at the time and was understandably unsure of exactly what happened but had seen his Lieutenant wounded in the head and felt it was from one of the German bombers' grenades. However, he did add, 'I saw his dead body lying in the trench.' Unfortunately Harry was taken prisoner and held until the end of the war, his statement only being given in March 1919.[16]

Both statements, however, were eclipsed by that of a medical officer's orderly who, just seven weeks after the event whilst on leave in Boulogne, provided information which leaves no room for doubt. By this time Keith's body had evidently been found. Sergeant Clownes states that Keith had been shot in the head with a bullet and that a cross had been prepared to put on his grave. Lieut. Milsom's fate was less clear, though his body was badly burned, and both officers had been buried together, 'in the burying place in Sanctuary Wood where a number of others of the 8th Rifle Brigade are buried'[17].

On 19 September, at a memorial service to Sidney Woodroffe, posthumously awarded the Victoria Cross for his part in an afternoon counter-attack at Hooge, the Master of Marlborough College delivered a sermon with a tribute to Keith summarising the essence of the man for those who still hoped that he may have been taken prisoner:

> We greatly fear, though there is still a dim hope, that Keith has gone. He was last seen driving the Germans from a trench and his many acts of bravery in going to pick up wounded were the talk of his company. He won the hearts of men as he won ours here, and those of his boys of Balliol Club at Oxford. His personality took men by storm. He was essentially a man who came not to be ministered unto, but to minister, and I fear he has given his life. God grant it may not be so!

Sadly, it was.

In gaining a clearer picture of those final moments of Keith's life, it is worth reconsidering Rifleman Griffiths' statement where he reveals regret at having to leave his officer behind. However, it also reveals that he and others of the platoon were retiring along Trench G5 whilst Keith stayed in position, firing at the enemy approach. He would have had but an instant to take the measure of the moment and decide what he would do. His path was clear. He would make a fighting stand, even though it was equally clear that he would be overrun and that such resistance would be futile and ultimately fatal.

That decision was both courageous and instinctive but may well have encompassed the considered fact that his actions would also benefit his men with an increased chance for survival, which in Griffiths' case certainly proved successful. Keith had always led by example in service to others. Never was this more apparent than in this, the manner of his death, in which he gave his final and greatest gift of service to his men, his God, his king and country; well might his epitaph be written: 'Well done, thou good and faithful servant.'

PURISTAN

They who, their cartridges spent, cut up, surrounded and beat
Fight back at fate till the end, scorning both death and defeat,
Who, though they know in their hearts that their resistance is vain,
Stand to the ground that they hold for that their duty is plain,
Who, at the end when the foe bids them surrender or die,
Die in the pride of their hearts, doing their duty thereby:
They have attained the ideal, their souls climb heaven. Their eyes
Pierce thro' the dream to the real; they have attained Paradise.

Capt. Claude Templar, 1st Battalion The Gloucestershire Regiment

Keith Rae's Memorial in 1921 sited where Trench G5 joined to the right of Hooge Crater.

Killed in action 4 June, 1918.

In spite of Sergeant Clownes' September 1915 account stating that Keith's body was buried, the Rae family were not aware of their son's fate and were left writing to the War Office and The Red Cross in search of information. A letter to the former in May 1919, from Keith's brother Charles, reveals that the family still hoped that he might be alive, perhaps 'severely maimed or mentally affected' in a home or hospital somewhere. From the wording of a dedication service held on Whit Sunday 1921 honouring a memorial to Keith at the site of the crater's edge,[18] it seems his status was still that of 'missing in action, believed killed'. It was as if his body's retrieval, identification and burial had never taken place and yet he, along with Milsom and Pawle, had been buried with others from the battalion.

The army's meticulous care with regard to the loss of any officer raises the question: as they must have been aware of what happened to his body, why did they not inform the family? Knowledge of a marked grave, which may not have survived the war, would at least have given the family 'closure' together with the solace of knowing

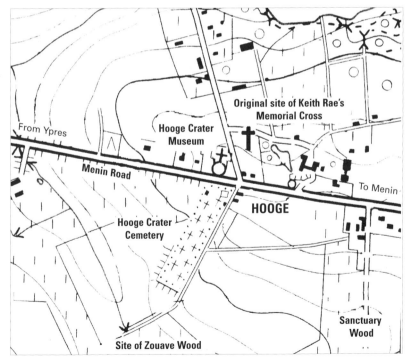

The original position of Keith Rae's Memorial Cross at Hooge.

that Keith had received a decent Christian burial.

Notes:

1. 2nd-Lieut. Stephen Reiss, 5th Royal Berkshires, killed on 13 October, 1915 is commemorated on the Loos Memorial to the Missing. He left money in his will for the use of the Balliol Boys Club. Lieut. Ronald Poulton Palmer, 1/4th Royal Berkshires was killed on 5 May 1915 and is buried at Hyde Park Corner [Royal Berks] Cemetery, Ploegsteert. His grave marker cross is mounted on the eastern wall of Holywell Cemetery, Oxford. The Keith Rae Trust, set up in 1921 by the Rae family in his memory, provided new premises for the Boys Club: Keith Rae House, plus an annual exhibition grant for an Old Marlburian at Balliol.The house was sold in 1971 when the club closed. The proceeds, invested by the Trust Fund is still used to support local Youth Club work in the city of Oxford..

2. Capt. A Adam, 1st Cambridgeshires, died of wounds in enemy hands 16 Sept. 1919 and is buried in Achiet-le-Grand Communal Cemetery Ext. France.

3. Of Keith's Common Room colleagues who were killed: Capt. Atkey, 9th Yorks, 5 July 1916, is buried in Bècourt Military Cemetery, Bècordel-Bècourt, and Capt. Wace, 5th Royal Berkshires, killed 3 July 1916, is commemorated on the Thiepval Memorial, France.

4. Also commissioned into the 8th Battalion from Marlborough College with Masters Rae and Gurner at the end of Michaelmas Term in December, 1914, were pupils Sidney Woodroffe and Albert Hooker. Woodroffe deliberated between his responsibilities to the school as Senior Prefect and his responsibilities to his country. Gurner wrote of Keith as a 'great-hearted idealist who saw, long before most of us, through the hollowness of much of the emotionalism that swept the school as it swept the country.'

5. Common ground existed between officers through Oxford links. At Balliol, Billy Grenfell, 2nd son of Lord Desborough and brother of the poet Julian, was a central figure in the Annandale Society whose values and boisterous behaviour Keith deplored. As brother officers, the two made reparations to their friendship.

6. Gen. Sir Neville Lyttelton, G.C.B, was uncle to chaplain Neville Talbot and his younger brother Lieut. Gilbert Talbot, 7th Rifle Brigade. His sister, Lavinia, had married Edward Talbot, Bishop of Winchester, at whose official residence, Farnham Castle, this inspection took place.

7. Lieut. Hooker's wound undoubtedly saved his life. He survived the war as did Capt. Bowlby, wounded during the 10 day occupation at Railway Wood, whose gunshot wounds to his right arm and left wrist left him partially disabled for life.

8. Rifleman John Cooper, aged 22, from Sloane Square, London, is commemorated on the Menin Gate, Ypres. His grave was probably lost under later shellfire.

9. The battalion felt its first officer death keenly but perhaps no one more so than Col. Maclachlan, a close friend of Cuthbert Balleine who was Sub-Rector of Exeter College, Oxford before the war. Capt. Balleine was buried, together with Corporal Duncan and Rifleman Tillet, at the dressing station on the Menin Road next to the mill and the Ecole de Bienfaissance where Woodroffe helped take them. After the Armistice the cemetery was moved in entirety to Bedford House, Zillebeke and forms virtually all burials of today's Enclosure No. 2.

10. The crater at Hooge was blown by the 175th Tunnelling Company on 19 July just prior to the 7th R.B.'s 10-day period of occupation. It was in-filled later in the war.

11. This fact, mentioned in almost every account of the morning's events, was the main indicator of the imminent attack. The sector had previously been subjected to a deluge of shelling, the intensity of which would have seriously hampered British scouting and reconnaissance - a factor vital in the enemy's need for secrecy both in his installation of 'liquid fire' equipment and increased troop activity.

12. 2nd-Lieut. Albert Wollinsky was killed in action 11 July 1916 at Fort Vaux, Verdun. He has no known grave.

13. Whilst organising the retirement in Trench G3, Foss Prior was wounded in the shoulder. By January 1916 he was fully recovered, but was killed on 15 September on the Somme. He is buried in Bernafay Wood British Cemetery. His body was recovered by his friend Capt. Sheepshanks. The 1/8th Sherwood Foresters' War Diary corroborates the starting point of the attack to be 'the line held by C Company.' It was the highest observation point in the line.

14. Both flanks fought hard in the face of overwhelming odds. On the right, the KRRCs held isolated positions for most of the day before withdrawing. To the left, in Trench G10, Sidney Woodroffe stalled the enemy advance, enabling his men time to retreat to safety. He reported back to HQ with his men later that morning before being killed in the afternoon leading a counter-attack. One of the men killed that morning, probably somewhere in Trench G5 near Keith, was his bugler Rifleman Blake, from Sheffield, who had run out with him to help with the wounded Royal Engineer. He is commemorated on the Menin Gate, Ypres, Belgium.

15. According to Capt. Sheepshanks, Keith's body was still missing, along with that of Lieut. Milsom, on the 16 August. The only available information was that of Rifleman Griffiths who had survived the ordeal and was probably wounded in the retirement from G5. His testimony, echoed by his formal statement, has been used frequently in portraying Keith's last stand. Griffiths, who survived the war, was described by Keith as being the 'author' of the phrase, 'on the Bible I swear'.

16. No officers were taken prisoner. Of NCOs and riflemen taken: the official German figure is just 19 captured by 4.30 am when the attack objectives were secure. Rfn. Harry Rogers spent the war at Limberg P.O.W. camp, Germany. Also taken prisoner was Rfn. Bernard Britland, wounded in both legs in Trench G5 and sent to the same camp after 3 months in a German hospital. Although Britland's friend Ted Wyatt was wounded right next to him, such had been the confusion in Trench G5, that Britland wrote to his mother twice from the camp to find out what had happened his friend. Britland eventually received a postcard from Wyatt 4 months later – he had survived and hadn't been taken prisoner.

17. Capt. Pawle's body was seen at the crater after the lines were retaken on 9 August. His body was the first located of the 3 missing officers from Trench G5. The only bombing party member to escape was Corporal Saxby who said in an interview that the entire party was lost when the Germans cut them off. On 23 March, 1918 he was taken prisoner, joining his fellow C company comrades in the Limberg P.O.W Camp where he died of pneumonia 3 days after the Armistice. He is buried in Berlin South Western Cemetery.

18. Although not where Keith was killed, his family chose the junction of the crater's edge and Trench G5 to erect a memorial in his memory. The dedication service in 1921 was led by the Chaplain of Talbot House, the Reverend P. B. Clayton. The inscription was chosen by Edward and Margaret Rae: "Christ's faithful soldier and servant unto his life's end." The memorial was moved to a spot outside the boundary wall of Sanctuary Wood Cemetery in 1966 (see page 12).

Officers of the 8th (Service Battalion) Rifle Brigade, 14th (Light) Division. 2nd-Lieut. S. C. Woodroffe (5th from right back row) was awarded the V.C., his brother Capt. L. Woodroffe (2nd left seated) the M.C., and Capt. A. C. Sheepshanks (3rd from right, seated) the D.S.O. for the parts they played in the action of 30 July 1915. Lieut.-Col. R. C. Maclachlan, the battalion's commanding officer is seated (with walking cane) in the centre of the photograph.

*A whistle blows ... There they go, as steadily as any rifle charge that was ever made, out of the wood, into the pitiless open on this glorious summer's afternoon. Officers, scarcely more than boys, are leading them, stick in hand. They are swept away, row upon row, by the scythe of The Reaper.*
Taffy Evans

3
LAMBS TO SLAUGHTER
Disaster at Hooge – 2.45 pm, 30 July 1915
41st Brigade, 14th (Light) Division.

THE GERMANS first introduced 'liquid fire' as a weapon against the British, in the early morning of 30 July 1915. It was used as a surprise opening ploy in a well-planned, efficiently executed attack on British trenches at Hooge on the Menin Road 2½ miles east of Ypres.

Launched against troops of the 8th Battalion Rifle Brigade and 7th Battalion King's Royal Rifle Corps, both of 41st Brigade, 14th (Light) Division the attack proved a complete success for the attackers and a total disaster for the defenders. The latter suffered casualties they could ill-afford, and lost what little high ground the British held in a critical sector of the Ypres Salient. The Germans, apart from retaking the ground they had lost during a British attack on the 19th of the month, had gained strategically important ground and unobstructed observation over Ypres. They had to take the town in their quest to reach the Channel Ports, their ultimate goal in this sector of the Western Front. This attack came only 3 months after their territorial gains following the gas attack opening of Second Ypres on 22 April.

The British regrouped and counter-attacked, but without success. With little planning, and ignoring advice from senior officers in the line, divisional command ordered another counter-attack for 2.45 pm that afternoon.

Using the same troops who were ousted from their trenches in the morning attack, together with the two weary battalions they had relieved the night before – all of them untrained in both bombing and counter-attack tactics – it was doomed to fail from its outset.

Artillery support was minimal, a 45-minute bombardment before the counter-attack was to be launched – just 45 minutes of shelling a position held by an enemy who had been afforded 12 hours to consolidate and prepare for just such an attack. It is doubtful if any thought had been given to the inevitable enemy counter-attack that would have been launched had, by any ghost of a chance, the British troops re-occupied their line.

35

As it was, the bombardment was partially successful in that shells that fell behind the newly occupied trenches destroyed more of the already damaged trench system. By the morning of the 31st, the enemy troops manning the new front were almost out of ammunition and supplies, cut-off from their supports and with no means of escape. Unfortunately, little damage was done to what was now the enemy front line as most of the shelling fell in front of it.

A full 41st Brigade operation, the frontal attack was to be led by the 8th RB, from Zouave Wood with the 7th RB in support. To their right the 7th KRRC, supported by the 8th KRRC, would attack from the trenches edging Sanctuary Wood. Having spent ten long days in the trenches suffering constant attack and taking heavy casualties before their relief the night before, the 7th RB and 8th KRRC had marched back to rest camps only to be recalled after an hour's rest, two at most, to help hold the new line taken up following the morning attack. Also depleted in strength and exhausted, having had no sleep or food for 36 hours, they were to take more casualties from enemy bombardment as they moved back into support lines in Sanctuary and Zouave Woods. To the left, The Culvert sector, the 9th KRRC of 42nd Brigade would attack with the 9th RB (also of the 42nd) in reserve. The 6th Duke of Cornwall's Light Infantry of 43rd Brigade was to be in reserve in Zouave Wood. The frontal battalions (battalions in name but certainly not in strength) were to cut through their own barbed wire to clear their path up a slope in full view of well-manned, infantry and machine-gun defended trenches a few hundred yards away. To make matters worse, the enemy expected, and had spent 12 hours getting ready, for such an attack.

Capt. A. C. Sheepshanks, commanding D Company, 8th RB, the only full company in the battalion, was to attack on a two platoon front from a position in front of the British wire, a position to be taken up during the 45 minute British bombardment.[1] The remnants of A and B Companies were to operate on his left (C Company was virtually non-existent having taken the brunt of the morning attack). Meanwhile Lieut.-Col. R. Maclachlan, C.O. 8th RB, arranged with the 7th RB that it follow in support as soon as the attack began.

Capt. A. C. Sheepshanks.

Like lambs being driven to slaughter, the troops attacked and, as with the lambs, they had no chance of survival. They were shot down in droves as soon as they left cover and, at 3.15 pm, the abortive attack was called off.

The results were as predictated by officers in the line. The frontal attack from Zouave Wood was a complete failure, making little or no headway against devastating machine-gun and rifle fire.

From The Culvert the 9th KRRC gained ground, but took heavy casualties, amongst them it's C.O. Lieut.-Col. C. S. Chaplin. The battalion was reinforced by a platoon of the 9th RB to hold the ground before successfully holding off an enemy counter-attack.

So ended a much-too-late, ill-advised, ill-prepared, under-manned attack, imposed upon, and against the advice of, senior

Lieut.-Col. C. S. Chaplin.

regimental officers by a command that thought it knew better whilst comfortably 'entrenched' some miles away. It was an attack that was doomed to failure at its time of conception.

The results of the German morning attack and the British afternoon counter-attack on 30 July meant more than the loss of a critical

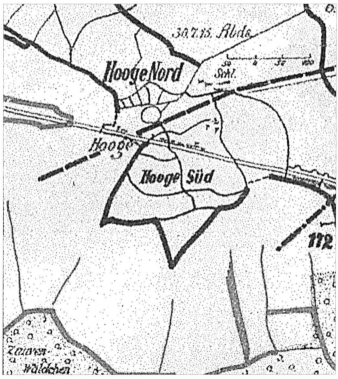

The German consolidated line, the objective of the British counter-attack at 2.45 pm in the afternoon of 30 July 1915 ( Map from 'Infanterie Regiment 126 in the World War').

sector of the Ypres Salient. The real cost was the casualties taken by those battalions of Kitchener's New Army in both the morning and afternoon attacks. Mostly volunteers who had only been in the war zone since the previous May, they had seen hardly three months of active service and, amongst the young and not-so-young volunteers, the best of the Officer Training Corps from public schools, colleges and universities throughout Great Britain. Many were serving as officers, but a great many of them had chosen to serve in the ranks, the Rifle Brigade and King's Royal Rifle Corps being seen as the regiments of choice to many at the time.

On 30 July alone, 22 officers and 454 other ranks were admitted to Casualty Clearing Station No. 10 at Remi Sidings, Lijssenthoek. On the 31st it recorded another 25 Officers and 950 other ranks, and on the 1 August yet another 20 Officers and 490 other ranks were admitted. No. 44 Field Ambulance was still collecting the casualties from the Zouave and Sanctuary Wood areas on 6 August.

The cost to the 42nd Brigade was: 7th RB – 16 officers and 300 men; 8th RB – 19 officers and 469 men; 7th KRRC – 13 officers and 289 men; 8th KRRC – 10 officers and 190 men, killed, wounded and missing. The 9th Battalion KRRC of 41st Brigade suffered 13 officers and 333 men, killed wounded and missing.

Accounts from those who were lucky enough to survive compound the shortcomings and raise doubts on the judgement related to the attack. Maj. F. M. Crum, 8th KRRC, an officer who had served in many theatres of war, was to write:

... and now we were in for a real attack, and one in which I for one honestly felt there was no fraction of a chance of success; 800 to 900 yards across the open, up a glacis held by trenches, with no covering guns, and under an unholy bombardment from every kind of German gun, fired from every side into our salient ... It certainly seemed a case of good-bye to this world, but I only felt a kind of regret that it was not a show more likely to succeed... It made it harder because I knew our Brigadier had personally protested, and yet had received peremptory orders to counter-attack. Even if our men had taken the hill, how could they face the terrific 'crumping' which always follows and the inevitable counter-attack? Our good men, 36 hours without food or water, or rest, and no training with bombs and rifle-grenades"

... But the odds were too great. Our 45 minutes bombardment had done nothing to save us. At least four or five hours scientific bombardment was needed. The Germans had done splendidly. Without losing a minute they had brought machine-guns up to the captured positions, so that when we advanced there must have been from six to ten machine-guns. There was not a square inch of dead ground. The 7th Battalion led the attack; then came our four

Companies, the Colonel keeping two of them, and me myself in reserve. ...I crawled out to the edge of a wood and saw what I could, and kept telling the Colonel that I could only see men being shot down, and could see no progress of the attack. ...The fire of the Maxims was terrific; nothing could live in the open near the edge of the wood. Few got far beyond the wood, and the wood itself was an inferno. From East, from North and from South, every kind of gun showered down shells and explosions. ...the Rifle Brigade met the same fate as ourselves. At about 3.30 Colonel Green, seeing no sort of hope of success, decided not to send in his reserves and to report that the attack was stuck up. Again I believe the Superior Authority from some spot miles away wished to attack again, but Oliver Nugent protested again, as also another Brigadier...

To succeed, a counter-attack must be instantaneous. You can't give an enemy twelve hours to defend himself and then attack him in a minority with tired troops. On the other hand, if you can't do it at once, you may have to attack, and then it is a case of clear thinking, careful reconnaissance and planning, superior numbers, every man his objective, fit and worked up, to enthusiasm; then, if well led, an attack succeeds...

An officer wounded in the morning attack spent the day lying out in the open from where he had an eyewitness view of the afternoon attack. He reported:

Without rest, food, or water for thirty hours they come back in broad daylight to retake – with scarcely any artillery preparation – the lost trenches, aided by the 9th Battalion of the KRR. All to no purpose - the Staff, it seems, have not yet learned that for a counter-attack to be successful it must be made within six hours and then only with artillery preparation to break down wire. The Brigadier knows what this will mean, but his protest is in vain.

Of his part in the attack Rifleman Strange Boston, 8th RB, wrote:

The noise overhead from the aeroplanes, the bursting shrapnel, the HE bombs and mortars was so deafening that one could not hear one's own voice.... I heard Lieut. McAfee shout: "We're going to charge when I whistle." He whistled loudly and, laughing at us, ran forward yelling, "Come on – come on you." We ran forward with the bayonet – firing dropping – firing and dropping again. There was a mighty roar that made the ground tremble, a burst of flame, a hail of earth, tree stumps, iron, explosives and, with thumping heart, I saw McAfee topple over. I don't know what hit him. I think a machine-gun got him.

Lieut. L. A. McAfee.

L/Cpl. D. Hankey.

L/Cpl D. Hankey, 7th RB was wounded in the thigh during the approach through Zouave Wood. Under his pseudonym *A Student In Arms,* his article, *The Honour of The Brigade,* was published in *The Spectator,* December 1915 recording:

Before them raged a storm. Bullets fell like hail. Shells shrieked through the air, and burst in all directions. The storm raged without abatement... A man went into hysterics, a pitiable object. His neighbour... perfectly, fatuously cool... A whistle blew. The first platoon scrambled to their feet and advanced at the double... They disappeared. The second line followed, and the third and fourth... No one hesitated. They went forward mechanically... the storm of lead and iron which met them mowed them away... the edge of the wood – choked with corpses...

Capt. L.Woodroffe.

Capt. L. Woodroffe, D Coy. 8th RB, moved along the communication trench to a point in front of the British wire. At 2.30 pm., 15 minutes prior to the attack launch time he breached the left wall of the trench and led his men out, deciding to move along the wire for 160 yards to allow them room to clear the trench. They were greeted with an onslaught of rifle and machine-gun fire the minute they left. Woodroffe counted every single, tortuous, stumbling 160 steps before throwing himself flat to catch his breath. He then began to crawl back to take a position in the middle of his line and was hit in the thigh, then a ricochet hit his knee, a bullet his boot heel and another went through his pocket. He tried to get to his second-in-command 2nd-Lieut. G. W. 'Billy' Grenfell but could not make it. He gave his whistle to a Corporal Carson to pass it on to Grenfell with instructions to lead the charge.

2nd-Lieut. G. W. Grenfell.

He then lay down with his head partly in a shellhole. He was to lie there for six hours, every hour taking a bite from an apple he had with him before, at 9 pm, dragging himself backwards to the British line.[2]

At 2.45 off they went, Grenfell leading with his glasses hanging half off, sprinting, his fists clenched, towards the enemy. Platoon-Sgt. Jackson saw him hit by a bullet in the head and another in the side, killed instantly. During clearing operations, Grenfell's body was found by Sgt. Rogers (C Coy. 3rd RB) in a row of others. The body was not identifiable owing to German sniping during the period it lay in No-Man's Land. Later his identity disc was found on him by Cpl. Lawrence, also of C Coy. 3rd

RB. He was buried on the spot. The map reference siting his grave clearly indicates that he and his men had only managed to advance a few yards north of the British wire.

2nd-Lieut. S. C. Woodroffe, A Coy. 8th RB, younger brother of Capt. Woodroffe, with a cheek wound covered with a field dressing held in place by a bandage around his jaw, left the trenches leading his men in the uphill charge. He was hit three times on his way to the wire

2nd-Lieut. S. C. Woodroffe. and died attempting to cut a path through it.[3]

A sketch by Capt. L. Woodroffe showing where the trench wall was breached and the direction taken to take up position in front of the British wire.

An eyewitness recounts Woodroffe's efforts as:

> He staggers, wounded ... recovers, walks on ... he is hit again, but staggers forward - right up to the enemy's wire and begins to cut it. He falls, but struggles up ... he is cutting now with his one remaining hand ... he dies on the wire. That is Sidney Woodroffe of the Rifle Brigade, aged nineteen – destined to be the first V.C. of the New Armies. And among those who have fallen there is also Gilbert Talbot – destined, in dying, to pass on his name to a new generation.

At last it ends – this terrible slaughter. No one has faltered, but all are fallen. The attack is held. The dusk comes on. The wood is filled with wounded, dying, dead. They are everywhere

Lieut. Gilbert Talbot.

Lieut. Gilbert Talbot, 7th RB, with his platoon arrived at his position at the edge of Zouave Wood at 1.40 pm with just 16 men unwounded. At 2.45, less than an hour later, he led them into the attack and the same fate befell him as that of Woodroffe. He died within yards of his fellow officer, on the other side of the wire over which he had fallen whilst trying to cut through it. His servant, Rifleman Nash, attempted to save him but was himself wounded. An account of Nash's part in the charge reads:

Rifleman G. Nash.

> At 2.45 he blew the whistle which was the signal to charge - and at once the men (sixteen were now available) leapt out, and rushed forward, Gilbert, followed closely by Nash, whom he had told to keep near him, headed them a few yards on, with the words "Come on, my lads - this is our day!" Soon he came to the old British barbed wire, which he was beginning to cut, when he was hit in the neck and fell over the wire fencing. Nash, badly hit in the left arm at the same moment as his master, dashed forward, wrenched out his bandages and turned Gilbert gently on his back and tried to bind up the fatal wound in his neck. His blue eyes opened wide and he saw Nash and gave him a bright smile, then he turned a little over, and died. While Nash's right hand was on Gilbert's breast pocket to lay him down a bullet pierced the third finger (it was afterwards amputated) and went right through Gilbert's cigarette case and, he supposed, through his heart.[4]

Talbot's elder brother Neville, Senior Chaplain, 6th Division, attached to 3rd RB, was instrumental in finding the bodies of both his brother and Woodroffe. He was later to record:

Gilbert fell on the 30th July. I wasn't allowed by the 14th Divisional Headquarters to go up on the 31st but I managed to get up all right on the night of 1st August, two nights after he had fallen...

... Anyhow, the first time I tried, just about dusk, I got into No Mans Land, first found the body of young Woodroffe VC, and then found Gilbert's body. It was very hot weather, and, of course, the bodies were much affected by it, it was rather horrid. I took his cap-badge, and some things out of his pocket. There was nothing more that could be done that night, so I got back into a trench...

Chaplain Neville Talbot.

History has determined 30 July 1915 as 'The day the Germans first used liquid fire as a weapon against the British'. The use of it, as terrifying as it was to those facing it, served no more than as a surprise tactic, enabling an infantry movement behind its screen to be implemented effectively. The defenders fought hard, and had attempted to regain their positions, without success. Why then were those same troops, who suffered both the initial attack and the unsuccessful counter-attack, expected to take part in a deemed-to-fail action against the same trenches just 12 hours later – 12 hours so well used by an industrious enemy to fortify his new positions, and who had no intention of giving them back without a serious fight?

Those who fell that afternoon must have known their fate – it would have been crystal clear to them, and to their commanders, that their chances of success, even survival, were virtually non-existent.

They fell in a counter-attack which should never have taken place. Hindsight does not apply here. There was enough 'foresight' flying about at the time to have prevented the attack. Surely, even under the discipline of war, a combined effort by a Brigadier-General and 4 Lieutenant-Colonels commanding 4 inexperienced, under-strength battalions, operating in one of the worst sectors of the Western Front, would be heard if their protest was put emphatically, with supporting facts and knowledge of the ground. It would appear however, Division was not made aware of, or chose to ignore the arguments.

The ground today, even with its military cemetery, agricultural expansion and residential dwellings in place, is clearly not an area to consider such a poorly planned and lightly supported attack.

At 10 Downing Street on 3 August 1915, Lord Kitchener, dining with Mr. Bonar Law, Mr. Winston Churchill, Lord D'Abernon, Lord and Lady Desborough and others, while discussing the death of the Desboroughs' son Billy Grenfell in the counter-attack, stated that the British had themselves to thank for the failures in the war and:

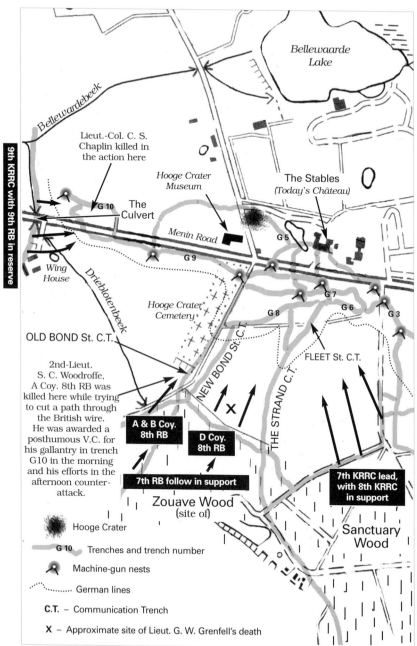

The area of the counter-attack as seen on today's map. Zouave Wood and Hooge Crater no longer exist, the former was never replanted and the latter was in-filled during the war. Hooge Crater Cemetery, Hooge Crater Museum and Wing House are shown as points of reference.

The Germans attack us and we wait to counter-attack them. This is madness, you must do it at once, while your enemy is exhausted, or, if you *can't* you should reform your plans with deliberation and slowly; but to wait, and then counter-attack impulsively, is to court disaster.

It would seem almost all involved (as well as others in higher places) believed the counter-attack should not have taken place.

On 2 August, just four days later, a seven day period of regular bombardment of the line around Hooge was begun. So orchestrated as to cause the enemy to think it was routine daily 'hate' shelling, it was coupled with diversionary tactics by the British 49th Division and the French XXXVI Corps feigning an attack to the left of the line. The 46th Division to the right, also simulated preparations for an attack. As planned, it misled the enemy into believing attacks were taking place elsewhere. Assuming that shelling on 9 August was another day's 'hate', they retired to their dugouts. Then Regular Army battalions of the 6th Division's 18th and 14th Brigades, with two RE Companies and two Trench Mortar Batteries attached, plus support from an RFC Squadron, attacked, quickly re-capturing the lost trenches together with another 500 yards or so of enemy territory.

That sort of thinking and planning four days before would have served well the 41st Brigade of 14th Division.

In his official report of 6 August, Brig.-Gen. O. Nugent D.S.O., A.D.C., commanding 41st Brigade wrote of the counter-attack:

... The position now occupied by the Germans formed a re-entrant with a glacis stretching from ZOUAVE WOOD to the MENIN road, devoid of any cover other than the woods in which troops could be formed up. I did not consider that a frontal attack to recover the trenches was practicable, and asked that the 42nd Brigade might be asked to co-operate on the South side of MENIN road.

The 9th Bn., K.R.R.C., of this Brigade were directed to co-operate, and the 6th Bn., D.C.L.I. belonging to the 43rd Brigade was lent to me as a reserve.

On reaching ZOUAVE WOOD about 11 a.m. I sent for the Commanding Officers and issued orders for a counter-attack to begin at 2.45 p.m. after a bombardment of three quarters of an hour.

... It was not possible owing to the dust to determine the effect of the bombardment on the trenches held by the Germans South of the Menin Road, but at 2.30 pm the Germans opened a heavy machine-gun fire on ZOUAVE and SANCTUARY WOODS, and during the bombardment they were seen standing in G8 with their rifles laid on the parapet.

The opinions of observers along the edge of the woods was that the fire was too much distributed and too far forward. ...

The track alongside today's Hooge Crater Cemetery runs partly along the site of the OLD BOND STREET communication trench

The site of the northern tip of Zouave Wood

The upward sloping ground over which the counter-attack took place

The edges of Zouave Wood from which the counter-attack launched

The ground today over which the 30 July 1915 afternoon counter-attack took place. The triangle of dark soil is where the northern section of Zouave Wood once stood. It was never replanted after the war's end. The crest of the upward slope is the Menin Road which housed along its northern and southern edges 9 German machine-gun nests, and another 3 edging Sanctuary Wood to the right (but out of sight) of the picture. The photograph was taken from Maple Avenue (Canadalaan) along the road to Sanctuary Wood Cemetery.

46

*'I did not consider that a frontal attack to recover the trenches was practicable'* clearly indicates his doubts – but he was overruled by Divisional command who decided that, without a counter-attack, the Zouave Wood position might become untenable.

He had asked to be reinforced by a complete division, plus extensive and lengthy artillery support, superior to that of the enemy without which he viewed 'the chances of success as desperate'. He settled for a minimum force of two battalions, and was given the 6th DCLI, 43rd Brigade and the co-operation of another, the 9th KRRC of 42nd Brigade, already in reserve to the 9th RB in the line at The Culvert. He then ordered the attack with an artillery support of only 45 minutes. What then were his thoughts on the chances of success?

Even if he had used these two battalions in the frontal attack, the results would hardly have been different, other than a higher casualty rate. Unobstructed machine-gun and rifle fire with uncut wire on upward sloping ground *'devoid of any cover'* does not differentiate between depleted or full strength units, nor 'fresh' or tired troops.

His observers were correct when describing the bombardment as being *'too much distributed and too far forward'*. Had it given more focus to the occupied trenches instead of the ground in front of them some chance would have been afforded the luckless attack force.

His report continues:

Precisely at 2.45 p.m. both attacks moved forward, and at once became the target for an intense machine-gun, artillery and 'Minenwerfer' fire. The artillery and 'Minenwerfer' fire was mainly directed on the Northern edge of the woods, and machine-gun fire swept the whole of the ground in front and appeared to be directed from the German trenches opposite G.1, from the wall, from several points along the MENIN road, from G.6, G.8, the junction of the STRAND and FLEET STREET, and from the upper end of BOND STREET.

The men showed no hesitation in following their officers; and the officers sacrificed themselves in a devotion to duty to which no words can adequately do justice... intensity of the fire was such that the men were swept away even before they could emerge from the woods.

... About 3.15 pm, being convinced that further attempts to reach the German trenches by frontal attack held out no prospects of success, I directed commanding officers to discontinue further attempts...

What else could have been expected when *'Precisely at 2.45 p.m. both attacks moved forward, and at once became the target for an intense machine-gun, artillery and 'Minenwerfer' fire'*? The Germans had had 12 hours preparing to do just that – and what else could have happened other than *'... intensity of the fire was such that the men were swept away even before they could emerge from the woods'*?

He was obviously correct when he considered the frontal attack impracticable, as indeed was just about every senior officer involved (all Regulars with tried experience in warfare). But, it took half-an-hour of senseless slaughter to convince himself that he was right.

Later that evening within Zouave and Sanctuary Woods, a strength of only 720 officers and other ranks could be mustered of the original 4,000 men of 41st Brigade.

*The Rifle Brigade History, Volume 1* writes of the attack:

The decision to counter-attack by day was taken against the advice of the Brigade Commander on the spot. "In my opinion," he wired to the Division, "situation precludes counter-attack by day. Counter-attack would be into a re-entrant and would not succeed in face of enfilade fire." But the Division, in overruling his objection, replied that if no counter-attack were made the Zouave Wood position might become untenable. They said it was essential to counter-attack as early as possible. The hour of 2.45 was chosen; and it was determined that the assault should be made by the Eighth Battalion attacking from Zouave Wood, and the 9th Bn. 60th attacking from The Culvert with the Seventh and Ninth Battalions Rifle Brigade in support. The objective was Hooge and the trenches in its neighbourhood. The attack, like almost every hastily improvised operation undertaken by either side during the whole war, was pre-doomed to failure. The utilisation, in the forefront, of a spent battalion that on the top of the heavy fatigue of a relief had been fighting throughout the remainder of the night, had obtained no rest, and had been without food and water since coming into the line was, to speak mildly, a serious error of judgment; for the quality of dash, so essential in such an operation, could hardly fail to be lacking.

*The Annals of the King's Royal Rifle Corps, Volume V,* noted:

... at 11.30 a.m., by order from the VI Corps, Major-General V. Couper made arrangements for an assault at 2.45 p.m. to recover the lost ground. It was to be carried out by both 41st and 42nd Brigades... ...after three quarters of an hour's bombardment by the divisional artillery and No. 2 Group Heavy Artillery Reserve – feeble indeed after the German tornado, but still, serving to encourage the assault – the 46th Division on the right and the 6th Division on the left co-operating by fire. The attack northward of the 41st Brigade, with the 6th Duke of Cornwall's Light Infantry of the 43rd Brigade (Brigadier-General G. Cockburn) attached, failed, not a man getting within 160 yards of the Germans; but the attack eastwards by the 9th K.R.R.C. of the 42nd Brigade succeeded in regaining part of the lost trenches.

It continues:

To the historian of the Great War the above is an account of a comparatively trivial incident of warfare, not affecting the general scheme; a small section of trench line lost and partly regained, with no effect in a tactical situation; at most another unhappy instance of useless loss of life owing to blind insistence by a higher commander, put of touch with the situation, in compliance with a hide-bound rule that every loss of ground must be met by an immediate counter-attack without any consideration of its chances of success; the result being losses to ourselves out of all proportion to those inflicted on the enemy, an unfailing way to lose a war of attrition if followed with sufficient obstinacy

An account published in *The KRRC Chronicle 1915*, reads:

The bombardment was ineffective; so much so that the Germans opened a heavy machine-gun fire from our recently held support trenches before the bombardment was at an end, and we could see the Germans standing up in the trenches themselves.

Nevertheless the counter-attack was launched at the appointed hour, 2.45 pm. The attack moved forward, the men behaved very well and the officers with a gallantry no words can adequately describe. As they came out of the woods the German machine-gun fire and shell fire met them, and literally swept them away line after line. The men struggled forward, only to fall in heaps along the edge of the woods.

[Interesting to note that *"the men behaved very well"*!]

Brig.-Gen. Nugent, D.S.O., A.D.C., was himself to say:

Led by their officers, each successive line swept forward and the last wave of men rolled forward from the woods with determined courage. The men literally fell in swathes, and headway was impracticable. First came a message from the left that one company only still remained. Shortly after, about 3.30 pm, the senior officer on the right reported that further progress was impossible. It was clear that the attack had been pressed home with a splendid gallantry and to its furthest limit, but that success was impracticable.

Nugent was later to write:

The curse of the salient had been heavy... Our losses great, Officers of a class we shall never be able to replace, the pick of English or Public School and 'Varsity life. Heroes in battle, they led their men with the most sublime courage, knowing, as I am certain they did, that they were going to certain death. The splendour of it! The glorious sacrifice of courageous lives in a noble cause! ... There is nothing but praise for the conduct of these young Battalions of the King's Royal Rifle Corps and The Rifle Brigade; nothing that you cannot relate with satisfaction and pride. They have had a fiery trial prolonged over nearly six weeks, culminating in the events of the 30th and 31st July 1915, and they have acquitted themselves worthily of the best traditions of the two great Regiments to which they belong.

Inspired wording, but to what avail?

'*The curse of the salient*' in this particular instance could only be the Command itself that thought it knew better, and '*knowing, as I'm certain they did, that they were going to certain death.*' is incomplete – it omits to mention that Nugent and the commanding officers of his battalions also knew without doubt that those company and platoon officers – not to mention the N.C.O.s and other ranks – '*were going to certain death.*'

'*The splendour of it! The glorious sacrifice of courageous lives in a noble cause*'? What was the 'noble cause'? It would seem that '*The glorious sacrifice of courageous lives*' was in itself the 'noble cause', and '*nothing that you cannot relate with satisfaction and pride.*' would better use the words 'guilt' and 'shame' in place of 'satisfaction' and 'pride'.

Those '*Officers of a class we shall never be able to replace, the pick of English or Public School and 'Varsity life*'' could well have lived to fight another day, as too would have the N.C.O.s and other ranks.

What then was the judgement of Second Army and VI Corps to the pointless loss of life to the 14th (Light) Division during that abortive counter-attack on the afternoon of 30 July 1915?

How did they compare the Division's decisions, preparation and tactics with the planning and implementation of the 6th Division's attack on 9 August, an attack which began its preliminary bombardment and diversionary operations a few days after 30 July?

Who was brought to account for such a wanton waste of life?

The Divisional Commander and the Regular Officers of 41st Brigade and its battalions, those who 'protested too little', then blindly followed orders and committed what was left of their officers and men to a counter-attack they knew must fail, were judged for their powers of leadership and responsibility of command as follows:–

Lieut.-Col. Maclachlan,
C. O. 8th Rifle Brigade

Lieut.-Col. Heriot-Maitland,
C. O. 7th Rifle Brigade

Brig.-Gen. Oliver Nugent D.S.O., A.D.C., Commanding 41st Brigade was promoted to Maj.-Gen. Commanding 36th (Ulster) Division in early September 1915;

Lieut.-Col. R. C. Maclachlan, C. O. 8th RB, was awarded the D.S.O. in 1916, promoted to Brig.-Gen., 112th Brigade, 37th Division in January 1917. He was killed by a sniper on 11 August 1917.

Lieut.-Col. J. D. Heriot–Maitland D.S.O, C.O. 7th RB, assumed command of 41st Brigade in September 1915, resumed command of the 7th RB later in the month and was appointed Brig.-Gen. 98th Brigade, 33rd Division on 1 September 1916.

Lieut.-Col. G. A. P. Rennie, D.S.O., C.O. 7th KRRC, Mentioned in Dispatches 1 January 1916 and promoted Brig.-Gen. 146th Brigade, 49th Division in October 1917.

Lieut.-Col. H. C. R. Green, C.O. 8th KRRC, Mentioned in Dispatches 1 January 1916 and awarded the D.S.O in June 1916. In July of the year took command of the 20th Brigade, 7th Division.

Maj.-Gen. V. A. Couper, Commanding 14th Division, the officer to whom the foregoing could have made a stronger protest against the counter-attack, the man, together with members of his Staff, who should perhaps have listened to those who knew better, was made a Knight Commander on 1 January 1918.

Maj.-Gen W. H. Greenly took over command of the 14th Division vice Maj.-Gen. Couper on 22 March but was ordered to take command of the 2nd Cavalry Division on the 27th. Maj.-Gen. Couper resumed command the same day but four days later, 31 March, he left to take command of a division in England.

Lieut.-Col. C. S. Chaplin, C.O. 9th KRRC, the only full strength battalion involved, was the sole commanding officer to take a part in the action and was killed whilst directing his troops.

Notes:

1. Capt. A. C. Sheepshanks was awarded the D.S.O. for the part he played in the action. With the exception of the war years, he was an assistant master at Eton from 1906 to 1938. He died on 4 April 1961.

2. Capt. L. Woodroffe, 31-years old, was awarded the M.C. He returned to the front on 1 June 1916 after recovering from his wound. He was wounded by shellfire the day he arrived and died of his wounds on 4 June. He is buried at Barlin Communal Cemetery Extension, France.

3. 19 year-old 2nd-Lieut. S. C. Woodroffe received a posthumous V.C. for his gallantry in both the morning attack and the afternoon's counter-attack. His name is commemorated on the Menin Gate memorial, Ypres.

4. Rfn. G. H. Nash was awarded the D.C.M. for his attempts to save the life of Lieut. G. W. Talbot.

**Second-Lieutenant Raymond Lodge**
2nd Battalion, The South Lanchashire Regiment.

*Our regiment was to lose many more on that same hill before the month was over, and those of us that remain are glad to be far away from it now; but I always feel that anyone who has died on Hooge Hill has at all events died in very fine company.*
A letter from Lieut. William Roscoe to Raymond Lodge's father: 16 May 1916

4
A GLIMPSE OF EVIDENCE
The Life and Death of 2nd-Lieutenant Raymond Lodge,
2nd South Lancashire Regiment, 7th Infantry Brigade.
Killed in action 14 September 1915.

I N NOVEMBER 1916 a publishing sensation of its day was launched. The title held the key to its widespread public appeal: *Raymond or Life and Death.* The book itself contained the after-death communication of a young infantry officer who had died of wounds on 14 September 1915, at Hooge, a small village east of Ypres in Belgium. Such was the level of interest in this subject that supplies of the book could not keep pace with demand and within six weeks of publication it was already into its sixth reprint. It is not difficult to understand why. As five months of fighting in the Somme battles had come to a close almost every family in the land had been touched in some way by the death of a loved one. The author of the book was the eminent scientist, Sir Oliver Lodge, who had spent most of his working life applying his professional skills to experiments investigating the paranormal. However, he had personal reasons for publishing *Raymond or Life and Death* and its message since the dead officer was 2nd-Lieut. Raymond Lodge, Sir Oliver's youngest son.

Born in 1889, on 25 January, Raymond was the youngest of six sons born to Oliver and Mary Lodge. The six sons were duly followed by his younger sisters, with Raymond occupying a favoured position as the 'baby' of his brothers and suitable for 'mothering' by the sisters. It appears the Lodge children enjoyed an extremely happy family life brought up by both parents respecting them as individuals, contrary to the norm of the time. Sir Oliver's scientific bias was complemented by Mary's artistic temperament, as she was an accomplished artist who had studied at The Slade School of Art.

Of all his children, Sir Oliver admitted to a deep affinity with his youngest son. The two were extremely alike in nature, interests and aptitudes: Raymond even sharing a similar speech impediment to his father when very young. He displayed an early passion for engineering and how things worked, leading him to progress from Bedales School to read engineering at Birmingham University where his father was now First Principal. After a two year senior engineering apprenticeship at the Wolseley Motor Works he joined the firm set up by his two older brothers Alec and Brodie who had taken up an idea of their fathers regarding electric spark discharge and founded the Lodge Plug Company, manufacturing spark plugs. Then war intervened.

In September 1914 Raymond was commissioned in the 3rd Battalion South Lancashire Regiment. Then, in March 1915, at little more than a moment's notice and as replacement for another officer, he was ordered to join a draft being attached to the 2nd Battalion at the front. On the 15th, Raymond caught a train from Birmingham to Euston Station in London and it is a mark of the family's close ties that three of his brothers travelled with him across London in order to wave him off from Waterloo Station as he headed for Southampton.

Within 10 days of joining the battalion, Raymond began writing home, providing a fascinating and unique insight into his experiences as junior officer of No.11 Platoon, C Company, 2nd South Lancs.

Almost immediately he wanted to let his family know where he was. Avoiding naming the town of Ypres in Belgium directly and also in an attempt to continue the family's tradition of word games he wrote:

Thank you very much for your letter wondering where I am. Very pressing are the Germans, a buried city.

The clue to his whereabouts was "a buried city", the name of that 'city' being 'buried' in the words "Very **pres**sing".

Raymond with his elder brother Brodie in the garden of the Lodge's residence in Edgbaston.

However, by 4 April, a redeployment of the brigade saw Raymond moved to Dickebusch and so he sent home an acrostic in order to inform them of his changed whereabouts:-

Lights  My first is speechless, and a bell
Has often the complaint as well.
Three letters promising to pay,
Each letter for a word does stay.
There's nothing gross about this act;-
A gentle kiss involving tact.
A General less his final 'K',
A hen would have no more to say.
Our Neenie who is going west
Her proper name will serve you best.

Whole  My whole, though in a foreign tongue,
Is Richard's name when he is young.
The rest is just a shrub or tree
With spelling 'Made in Germany.'

An acrostic is a poem where the solution to each line gives initials that spell out a word or phrase. Raymond's clever acrostic was successfully decoded by the family:

D umB
I   o  U
CaresS
K  lu C k
E  dit H

Raymond was pleased to find himself in the same company as both of his best friends from training: Lieutenants Thomas and Fletcher. Also in the company was a Private Raymond who provided an amusing incident relayed home for the family's entertainment:-

I was dozing in my dug-out one evening and the Sergeant-Major was in his, next door. Suddenly he calls out again 'Raymond!' I started. Then he calls out again 'Raymond! Come 'ere!' I shouted out 'Hall! What's the matter?' But then I heard the other Raymond answering, so I guessed how it was...

On 16 April during a cold, rainy night, Raymond trudged back to billets at Dickebusch from the fire trenches some distance away. It was the 'darkest night' he could remember and the single file of the company was halted frequently by the need to 'freeze' in its tracks as Very lights lit the sky. The journey, interspersed with negotiating obstacles along the way, induced a lengthy letter home discussing the exact workings of a Very light. For their part, the family evidently

The Lodge family photograph; Raymond is seated third from left in the front row.

endeavoured to scour contacts in order to procure various equipment and inventive prototypes to send him. There continued an exchange of ideas on how Very pistols could be improved if the barrels were made longer and there was also a request made for a plan of the stars, printed in *The Daily News* of 3 April, which Raymond had seen and asked for to improve his night-orienteering skills on working parties.[1] The last day of April saw the battalion redeployed between billets at Ridge Wood and Elzenwalle Château. Raymond now found himself billeted in the old château, and his delight at his impressive surroundings is obvious:-

> I wish you could see me now. I am having a little holiday in Belgium. At the moment I am sitting in the shade of a large tree, leaning against its trunk, writing to you. The sun is pouring down and I have been sitting in it lying on a fallen tree, but it makes me feel lazy, so I came here to write (in the shade). Before me, across a moat is the château – ruined now, but not by old age.

This letter, dated 30 April, also provides a highly detailed, almost architectural, description of the design and construction of the château together with a layout of its overgrown gardens. This same letter also goes on to reveal that the young lieutenant was already utilising his engineering skills and that, because of it, the battalion's C Company was gaining a burgeoning reputation as first-class pioneers:

> ... had great fun arranging a 'source' in my trench ... A little stream, quite clear and drinkable after boiling, runs out at one place (at about 1 pint a minute!) and makes a muddy mess of the trenches. By damming it up and putting a water-bottle with the bottom knocked in on top of the dam, the water runs in a little stream from the mouth of the bottle. It falls into a hole large enough to receive a stone water-jar, and then runs away down a deep trough cut beside the trench. Farther down it is again dammed up to form a small basin which the men use for washing; and it finally escapes into a kind of marshy pond in rear of the trenches.

C Company officers had given Raymond the honorary position of 'O.C. Works'. Fellow officer, Lieut. Fletcher, had been an architect in civilian life and between them major improvements wherever possible were regularly undertaken as a matter of course.

On 6 May the battalion carried out pioneering work at Hill 60. It occupied trenches near the crest of the hill improving them, digging new positions, constructing water supplies and latrine saps under the guidance of the Royal Engineers and burying the many British and German casualties from the recent fighting.[2] During this period the battalion diaries refer to Raymond's fellow officer Lieut. Fletcher who on 9 May was the last in a series of officers and men wounded by shelling. Though able to continue with his duties at the time, by the

18th Raymond wrote home with regret that his good friend had:

> ... gone off for a rest cure... his nerves are all wrong and he needs a rest.

Obviously suffering from shell shock, some incident had apparently occurred, discussed by both men two days later when Raymond visited his friend in hospital:

> He does not read, he does not even walk about the grounds. He cannot sleep much and he said he did not know exactly *what* he did. He sees all the past horrors all over again; things which, at the time, he shut his mind to.[3]

June came, and with it a month of incident and further loss for Raymond. The battalion was now employed almost solely in pioneer work. On the 2nd, C Company dug 250 yards of support trench in one night alone, just behind Railway Wood alongside the Ypres-Roulers railway. The following night it constructed a communication trench further down the railway, from the GHQ line south of Hellfire Corner across to the Ecole de Bienfaissance. In between these nightly working parties, daily musketry training and drill took place. This was an unfortunate by-product of the C.O.'s vigorous enthusiasm to uphold the battalion's growing reputation. Raymond commented on his fear that 'they will wear us all out and the men as well'.

On the night of 7 June, Capt. Salter, B Company Commanding Officer, was killed at the end of a night's trench improvement in Sanctuary Wood. Salter was in charge of the B and C Companies' working parties. Raymond wrote that they were just about to leave the sector when the captain was shot through the head and killed instantly. His men buried him where he fell, by the side of a path at the edge of the wood.[4]

After a couple of days near Vlamertinghe testing new gas mask issues, the battalion received orders to participate in preparations for an imminent attack at Bellewaarde. They were to dig assembly trenches at Witte Poort Farm and Y Wood – and the attack was only four days away.[5] Owing to the exposed position all work was carried out without respite under rifle and shellfire.

After 3 nights the assembly positions were finished by midnight on the 16th, just two hours before being occupied by the 7th, 8th and 9th Infantry Brigade assault units in readiness for the attack at 4.15 a.m. The tired 'pioneers' returned to the Ypres town walls, waiting in reserve whilst assisting in the reception and dispersal of any German prisoners. Raymond writes of them:

> Poor devils, I do feel so sorry for them. One officer of 16 with six weeks service. Old men with grey beards too, and many of the student type with spectacles – not fit to have to fight.

By 9 p.m. the battalion was ordered back to the newly captured positions held by units of the 8th Brigade in order to consolidate. Not surprisingly for the first day of a battle hastily conceived, planned or prepared across three brigades, the battalion diary states:

> On arrival at the position there was a certain amount of confusion amongst the units in occupation and it was found impossible to carry out the work intended.

It was during this 'confusion' that Raymond's other close friend Lieut. Thomas was killed. Raymond wrote on 21 June:

> ... the whole battalion was ordered out digging to consolidate the captured positions. We got half-way out, and then got stuck – the wood being blocked by parties of wounded. We waited on a path alongside a hedge for over an hour and though we could not be seen we had a good deal of shrapnel sent over us. To make matters worse, they put some gas shells near, and we had to wear our helmets though the gas was not very strong. It was exceedingly unpleasant and we could hardly see at all. It was while we were waiting like this that Thomas got knocked out.

Thomas had been talking to the captain of the company behind when a piece of shrapnel caught him on the head and, though taken back to the dressing-station further down the Menin Road, he died of wounds about an hour later. He never recovered consciousness. In a self-confessed 'trance' at the shock of Thomas's death, Raymond wrote immediately to his friend's mother explaining what had happened and, in an extraordinarily compassionate paragraph, revealed the reverence with which her son's effects have been packed and sent home:

> It made my heart ache this afternoon packing his valise; I have given his chocolate, cigarettes, and tobacco to the Mess, and I have wrapped up his diary and a few loose letters and made them into a small parcel. The papers and valuables which he had on him at the time will be sent back ... the other things, such as letters, etc., in his other pockets I have left just as they were. I hope the valise will arrive safely. He will be buried very simply, and probably due east of Ypres about ¾ of a mile out – near the dressing station. I will of course see he has a proper cross.[6]

On 16 June, Raymond had received news that he had been approved for the position of battalion Machine Gun Officer. Ten days later he found himself at GHQ Machine Gun Training School in the convent outside St. Omer. 16 days of training, or 'my little holiday' as he put to it, came to an end with an added bonus of five days home leave spent in England with the family before rejoining the battalion in late July as assistant to Machine-Gun Officer Lieut. Roscoe.

Working in shifts with Roscoe and back in the St. Eloi sector, Raymond began working on a mounting for firing at aeroplanes, and also a device for automatic traversing.

Most of August was spent in the Dickebusch sector with an opportunity for the re-shaping of the battalion under newly-promoted Commanding Officer Lieut.-Col. Cotton.

Then, on 23 August, orders were received that 7th Infantry Brigade was to redeploy the following day to Hooge. Headquarters was established on the edge of Sanctuary Wood and, owing to a shortage of officers, Raymond found himself 'taken off machine-guns for the time being' and returned to Company duties. Working parties were required to improve and extend the front line Trench G5 in a northeasterly direction from the existing section at the Hooge Château stables. The new line would include Hooge Crater and all surrounding positions captured by the 6th Division's recent successful attack on 9 August.[7]

The battalion were also to extend a further front line in advance of The Stables, running parallel to Trench G5. The work was carried out on an exposed site in very close proximity to the enemy. Raymond describes the experience of this 'accursed neighbourhood':

We had to go up a trench which ran right out into space and which had only just been built itself, and when there we had to get over the parapet and creep forward to the new line we were to dig. Of course we had to be dead quiet, but there was a big moon, and of course they saw us. Most of the way we were not more than 30 yards away from their front position (and they had bombing parties out in front of that)... It was awful work, because they kept throwing bombs at us, and what was almost worse was the close-range sniping.

Amidst the debris Raymond struggled to find any safe ground:

The Germans were on the edge of a wood and our ground was tipped towards them, so it was extremely difficult to get cover. Very lights were going up from the German lines all the time, and you could see the bullets kicking up the dust all around. When we first got out there I picked out my ground pretty carefully before lying down (because the recent scrap there was much in evidence), but when the snipers got busy I didn't worry about what I was on, I just hugged the ground as close as I could. They would put the Very lights right into us and one just missed me by a yard. If they are not spent when they come down, they blaze fiercely on the ground, and when they finish they look like a little coke fire.

Then, after nearly six months active service, Raymond caught his first sight of a German adversary in the ghostly glare of a Very light:

Oh! I have seen my first German (not counting prisoners). I was standing up and a Very light went up, so I kept perfectly still. I was looking towards the wood where the Germans were (40 or 50 yards away) and I saw one quite distinctly walking into the wood.

C Company, under Company Commander Capt. Taylor, was selected to stay on in The Stables sector to work on the new trench position, returning to bivouacs southwest of Vlamertinghe on 4 September, being now temporarily attached to 8th Infantry Brigade.

On 5 September, something occurred which threw the full weight of responsibility onto Raymond. He was promoted acting Company Commander when Capt. Taylor sprained his ankle. A brief letter home the following day hoped it would not be for long: 'Too responsible at the present time of crisis'. It was indeed a brief promotion: on 12 September after a week at rest and a battalion inspection by General Plumer, Raymond returned to the Hooge sector for the last time.

On the morning of 14 September, A Company and three platoons of C Company garrisoned the newly-dug advance front line at The Stables. The artillery sent up word that there was going to be a bombardment and recommended a temporary front-line evacuation in case of retaliatory enemy strikes. At around 9 a.m. Raymond, as acting Company Commander, gave orders for C Company to withdraw back into Trench G5. He and fellow officer 2nd-Lieut. Ventris waited at the rear of the men as they withdrew, moving further down the trench to consult with the Company Sergeant Major. It was during these brief moments that a sudden enemy salvo arrived. As shards from the exploding shells were thrown into the air, Raymond's batman, Private Gray, received a fatal head wound, 2nd-Lieut. Ventris was killed outright and Raymond himself was hit in the back.[8]

Twenty minutes later, A Company officer, Lieut. Case, made his way to a nearby dug-out where Raymond had been taken:

I saw he was badly hit and tried to cheer him up. He recognised me and was just able to ask a few questions.[9]

However, by the time Machine-Gun Officer, Lieut. Roscoe, called at the dug-out, Raymond was already unconscious:

... I was going up the line to visit the guns, when I saw Ventris, who was killed, laid out ready to be carried down, and presently I saw your son in a dug-out, with a man watching him. He was then quite unconscious, though still breathing with difficulty. I could see it was all over with him. He was still just alive when I went away.

Three hours later Raymond died from his wounds. That evening the bodies of Lodge and Ventris were taken to the aid post at Gordon House near Hellfire Corner and buried side by side.[10] The battalion's Medical Officer, Capt. Cheves, wrote to the Lodge family that Raymond's wound was such that there had been no chance of saving his life, a fact 'recognised by all, including your son himself'.

On 17 September a telegram from the War Office informed the

Lodge household of Raymond's death. Just eight days later Lady Mary Lodge arranged a private psychic sitting for a friend with a Mrs Leonard, a medium at that time unknown to them. During this sitting a message was spelt out for Lady Lodge:

Tell father I have met some friends of his.

When asked who, the name 'Myers' was given. Following in the wake of a message a month previously from the same dead friend via an entirely independent medium in America, the family – although no strangers to the paranormal – were captivated.[11] So began many months of psychic sittings held mainly, though not exclusively, under the guidance of Mrs Leonard and published verbatim in *Raymond or Life and Death*. Sir Oliver's scientific approach and interposed comments to the transcripts provided a stamp of authority which was central to the impact of this book on a largely grieving public.[12]

Sir Oliver focussed on examining all communication as evidence. A central part was played by the mention of a photograph, unknown to the family. Described in great detail as being taken against vertical lines at the back, the key factor was that someone had lent on Raymond's shoulder. In late November the Lodges received a photograph of the Battalion officers from Capt. Cheves' mother: it matched every detail.

The book's third subtitle reflects the majority of its content: *'With Examples of the Evidence for Survival of Memory and Affection After Death'*. However, in considering 'examples of the evidence' the short opening section containing Raymond's selected letters is, by comparison, a revelation of the remarkable qualities of the human spirit. This is, perhaps in itself, a more convincing argument for the possibility of its continuance after death, expressed by 2nd-Lieut. John Glubb RE as he contemplated the dead at High Wood, September 1916:

One cannot see these ragged and putrid bundles of what once were men without thinking of what they were – their cheerfulness, their courage, their idealism, their love for their dear ones at home. Man is such a marvellous, incredible mixture of soul and nerves and intellect, of bravery, heroism and love – it *cannot* be that it all ends in a bundle of rags covered with flies. These parcels of matter seem to me proof of immortality. This cannot be the end of so much.

Notes:
1. With news in England of the gas attack at St. Julien, 22 April 1915, Raymond's letters contain reassurances that he had not encountered gas. In typical style the relative merits of various preventatives such as soda or ammonia were discussed.

2. Many of the dead were casualties of gas attacks on 1 and 5 May. 'Special sprayers

for use in driving gas out of trenches, together with a special solution' were issued to the battalion. On 12 May their war diary notes: 'The faces of the dead soldiers who were buried by our men were quite black and all metal work of their equipment was covered by a heavy green substance.'

3. Lieut. Fletcher didn't rejoin the battalion until after Raymond's death. He was killed in action on 3 July, 1916 in a retirement from positions near the Leipzig Salient. Fletcher is buried in Delville Wood Cemetery, Longueval.

4. Capt. Salter, killed, 8 June 1915, was buried in Sanctuary Wood. His body was found after the war, re-buried in Sanctuary Wood Cemetery and his name was erased from the Menin Gate.

5. Capt. Billy Congreve, 3rd Rifle Brigade writes of his dissatisfaction at the hurried nature of the attack: '... it is the most desperate business to get everything ready in four days. It is almost ludicrous and would be, if it wasn't so desperate; all the orders and reconnaissances to be done and a thousand other things.'

6. Lieut. Rittsen-Thomas died of wounds on 16 June 1915 and was buried at the Advanced Dressing Station, No. 9 Field Ambulance on the Menin Road. His body was exhumed after the war and re-buried in Ypres Town Cemetery Extension.

7. The extension of Trench G5 was still unable to advance the position beyond The Stables at its eastern end due to the proximity of the enemy. Billy Congreve explains:- 'The South Lancs have done first-rate work up in Hooge and we have now reached The Stables, but cannot dig a trench round the Boche side of it – as the latter has brought his trench up very close there.'

8. 2nd-Lieut. Ventris and Pte. Gray were the only other fatalities. Four were wounded, two of them seriously. Pte. Gray died from his wounds and is commemorated on the Menin Gate.

9. 2nd-Lieut. Case was killed 10 days later, on 25 Sept. 1915, in the Second Attack on Bellewaarde. He is commemorated on the Menin Gate.

10. The dug-out where Raymond died was somewhere along Trench G5 where C Company had withdrawn for the duration of the bombardment. He and 2nd-Lieut. Ventris were buried next to Gordon House but were exhumed after Armistice and moved to Birr Cross Roads Cemetery,

11. Myers had died in 1901. The message received was a reference to the classics which Sir Oliver interpreted as an impending blow through which Myers would provide some form of protection or support.

12. Sir Oliver's interest in the paranormal was influenced through his friendship with F. W. H. Myers, co-founder of the Society for Psychical Research of which Lodge was president from 1901-1903. In 1900 he was offered the position of First Principal of the University of Birmingham, the first of the modern civic universities to secure a charter. As a professional scientist in an age of discoveries like X-rays, electromagnetic waves, radioactivity and the electron, Lodge's counsel was sought by men of influence. Friends ranged from Elgar, G. B. Shaw, Sir Arthur Conan-Doyle to Keir Hardie. His contribution to the invention of wireless telegraphy includes being the first man to transmit a message by a wireless signal. His work with the nature of the ethersphere led him, in 1894, to hypothesise that the sun emitted radio waves, a fact not proven until after his death, in 1942. His lifelong friendship with Arthur Balfour brought him into contact with the elite of society through the group known as *The Souls*, of whom the Wyndhams were his closest friends. He received his knighthood in 1902.

In memory of Lieutenant-Colonel John Maxwell M.C. D.S.O.

*Clear on the first black night of war*
*Shone thro' the gloom a fair, white star,*
*Old Freedom's star that tyrants dread,*
*Beckoning and beaconing overhead,*
*Pointing the way that brave men tread;*
*He saw the star and followed it.*
*For three long years his path it lit,*
*By Ypres town, in Delville Wood,*
*Ever above his head it stood,*
*And, when he laid him down to die,*
*White with its glory was the sky.*
*O fair The Star, the star of bronze,*
*The Star of Ypres and of Mons,*
*But fairer far his old star that led,*
*The star that still shines overhead,*
*Gleaming down softly on the dead.*

John Bain
Assistant Master, Marlborough College.

*The world might stop in ten minutes;*
*Meanwhile, we are to go on doing our duty.*
*The great thing is to be found at ones post,*
*A child of God, living each day as if it were our last, but planning as though our*
*world might last a hundred years.*
C. S. Lewis

5

## 'FIGHTING JOHN': SOLDIER AND PATRIOT
### Lieutenant-Colonel John Maxwell D.S.O., M.C.
### 7th Battalion Rifle Brigade attd. 8th King's Royal Rifle Corps
### Died of wounds 4 December 1917.

W HEN A SOLITARY German shell came whining out of the night sky on 3 December 1917 at Meetcheele nearby the village of Passchendaele it brought to an end the life of the 8th King's Royal Rifle Corps Commanding Officer, 36-year old Major (acting Lieut.-Col.) John Maxwell M.C. Born 1 August 1881, John Maxwell was the eldest son of a family from Marlborough, Wiltshire who sent all three of its sons to Marlborough College. During one winter at the school John put up a notice at the foot of his bed stating: "Get up at once – don't funk!" Fellow-officer, Col. Lord Gorell, later remarked: "Throughout his life he obeyed the spirit of that notice".[1]

In March 1898 Maxwell left the college and subsequently studied at Keble College, Oxford where he gained a B.A. graduating in 1902. He worked with the Eastern Produce & Estates Company in Ceylon from 1907, receiving militia training with the Ceylon Planters Rifles. In the summer of 1914 he was back in England on holiday at the family home, then in Bath. The day war broke out he enlisted in nearby Taunton as a private in the Somerset Light Infantry. Within days he was commissioned and was gazetted on 9 September 1915, to the 7th Rifle Brigade, 41st Brigade, one of the first-formed of Kitchener's New Army. Within two months he was promoted to Lieutenant and in May 1915 went to France as signalling officer with the battalion.

After just 9 weeks Maxwell was to acquire a sobriquet that would recall the dark days of the end of July to those few who survived them: a period in the front line at Hooge followed by a single day, 30 July, saw most of the original draft of the 7th Battalion either killed or wounded. Fellow officer, Hon. E. J. Kay-Shuttleworth, listed Maxwell as one of only four officers to survive the day. Kay-Shuttleworth himself was wounded on his way out of Zouave Wood after the action. A shell burst in front of him just outside the wood, skinning his shin. He confessed to a momentary loss of self-control and reason. Maxwell came to his assistance and took charge as he and Kay-Shuttleworth's servant took the injured officer back to battalion headquarters.[2]

65

Maxwell's contribution to the day's battle earned him the title 'Fighting John' to which he would be known throughout the brigade. He was later promoted Captain and commanded the battalion's C Company for over a year. It was as the C.O. of C Company that Maxwell was happiest. In a tribute to him after his death by his friend Col. Lord Gorell, an insight is gained into his style of command:

> He was the servant as well as the leader of his men: at all times and in all places they came first in his thoughts, and until they were made as comfortable as circumstances permitted he gave no thought to himself. He was a strict disciplinarian, but so just and thoughtful in his discipline that his rule lay lightly, and the execution of his commands ran like a smoothly turning wheel. Every man, every officer in 'C' Company knew that he had only to be a 'trier' to have his commander an unfailing friend... It was not that he scorned comfort or luxuries but that he assessed them at their proper value. No one enjoyed a comfortable mess or jolly dinner more than he; no one put up more placidly with unavoidable discomfort. He enjoyed riding when the battalion was out at rest and he could make the time from the thousand and one calls upon his attention; but on the line of march he never rode, except to reconnoître or move up and down the line, and would turn out of the ranks at the end of the longest day, his figure erect, his step resilient, his long pole of English ash in his hand, his keen eyes taking in every detail of his company as it passed, his voice raised in that blend of personal exhortation and general command much made the onlooker realise both how intimately he knew his men and how his authority swayed them. The laggard closed up, the weary straightened, and into the village or camp which was its destination swung 'C' Company proud of themselves and their commander.

Autumn 1915 saw more action at Hooge in the Second Attack on Bellewaarde, followed by months of 'holding on' around Lancashire Farm, the Canal Bank and Essex Farm which 'chafed John's spirit' with its steady drain of men.[3] He was a front line commander, usually to be found, pipe in hand, undertaking his duties, calculating the risks and leading by example. Lord Gorell again elucidates:

> If, for instance, a piece of his line was being heavily shelled he went there at once, not obviously or with a trace of the heroical spirit, but in absolute simplicity to see if he could do anything, and at the least to be an encouragement to those who had no choice but to remain there. He took no undue risks; he knew that an officer's life is his country's, not his own, and was the first to condemn recklessness; but where he was wanted most, there, no matter what the conditions, he was always to be found, smoking his pipe calmly and doing all that was necessary or possible.[3a]

On 21 February the battalion left the Ypres sector, entraining from Cassel to Amiens, spending spring in the Arras sector before moving south to the Somme. In the King's Birthday Honours List, June 1916 Maxwell was awarded the Military Cross:

... for his untiring work since the foundation of the Battalion and for his exemplary and distinguished efforts since the Battalion came abroad.

On 12 June he was promoted Major. On 18 August his contribution to an action on the Somme earned him the additional title of 'Battling John'. On 1 September he was promoted second in command, his first major test being an assault on the southeast corner of the village of Flers on 15 September. The battalion performed well and his leadership was commented upon as being instrumental to the day's success. In the following spring, his conduct in the battalion's involvement in the Battle of Arras was such that a posthumous D.S.O. was awarded him in the New Year's Honours Gazette of January 1918

... for great gallantry, coolness and initiative on several occasions, notably during the Battle of Arras, April 1917 where at a critical moment he showed sound judgement and a power of leadership of the highest order.

Small surprise then when, on 10 September 1917, he was promoted to acting Lieut.-Col. and offered temporary command of the 8th King's Royal Rifle Corps, a sister battalion within the 41st Brigade then at Aldershot Camp, a rest and training area between Ravelsberg and Neuve Eglise. The following day the brigade relieved the 42nd at the front, and Maxwell, with little or no time to familiarise himself with his men and brother officers, led his new command into the line for a seven day stint of duty northeast of Messines.

On 17 September, after an uneventful tour of duty, the battalion was relieved – 'uneventful' included receiving a direct hit on battalion headquarters and a company outpost being raided which: '... caused a few casualties on both sides'. The brigade then went into reserve at Bristol Castle, a camp between the villages of Wulverghem and Messines. From there it returned to Aldershot Camp on the 21st where it spent the rest of September in rest and routine training.

Maxwell's October and November were fairly uneventful, seeing a short period in the line coupled with much training and movement from camp to camp. On 6 October the brigade moved from Aldershot Camp to bivouacs at Zevencoten from where, on the 11th, it moved into the line at Polderhoek. Relieved after five days, it moved to Ridge Wood Camp just north of Vierstraat and then, on the 22nd, to Chippewa Camp northwest of La Clytte. From there, on 23 October the

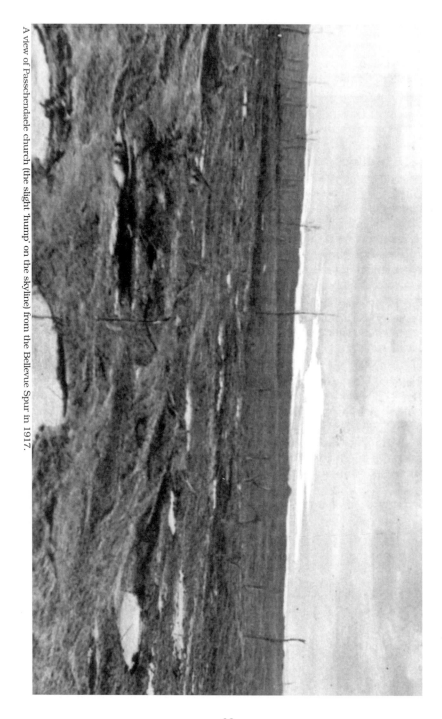

A view of Passchendaele church (the slight 'hump' on the skyline) from the Bellevue Spur in 1917.

68

move was to billets near Meteren in northern France. Here it remained until 11 November when it entrained for Tattingham, west of St. Omer for a period of intensive preparation for front line duty. This continued until 29 November when the brigade moved back to the Ypres Sector into B Camp, Brandhoek for final instruction. On 2 December it spent the day at California Camp north of Wieltje collecting battle stores before it went into the line to relieve the 25th Brigade at Meetcheele on the Bellevue Spur near Mosselmarkt, north of Passchendaele.

The three months of 'rest', training and a great deal of movement around Belgium and northern France had given Maxwell the time to get to know his company officers and men and to hone them into a fighting unit he would be proud to lead.

On 10 November, fighting in the Ypres Salient had closed down for the winter months. Units of the 1st Canadian Corps had secured the heights of the Passchendaele Ridge and both allies and enemy were suffering from the strenuous efforts employed to reach this point from the original July opening of the offensive. The Germans had lost a seemingly impregnable position around Passchendaele but could rest content, knowing that they had fought a retreat which had come close to exhausting the Allies. They were determined to hold onto a new winter line around the rest of the ridge and wait for firmer ground in the coming spring to win back the lost ground. British efforts had been expended in a torturous advance over a cratered wasteland, taking heavy losses as they went. Under Sir Douglas Haig's overall command they could only view the operation as a 'pyrrhic' victory, with victory and defeat almost blending into one. Not without cause was Passchendaele described: 'the most obscene battlefield in history'.

Although the many battles of Third Ypres had 'officially' closed down, the area in which Maxwell now found himself on 2 December was by no means quiet. This part of the line well known to the Germans, and particularly so their gunners. Passchendaele and its surrounds was a morass, a barren area of water-filled shellholes inter-dispersed with heavy, wet, shell-churned mud. Movement across it by man or machine was virtually impossible other than by what was left of the few usable roads. The only cover available was in the captured trenches and  enemy fortified buildings that were left standing – the pillboxes, troop shelters and strongpoints. The German gunners had everything well registered and were determined to ensure that the Allied troops on their new front were aware of who was facing them.

This then was the situation in which Maxwell and his battalion now found themselves. At about 9 pm on 3 December he, together with his orderly and signalling officer 2nd-Lieut. Woods, left headquarters at the once German occupied Bellevue Farm, a fortified strongpoint, to

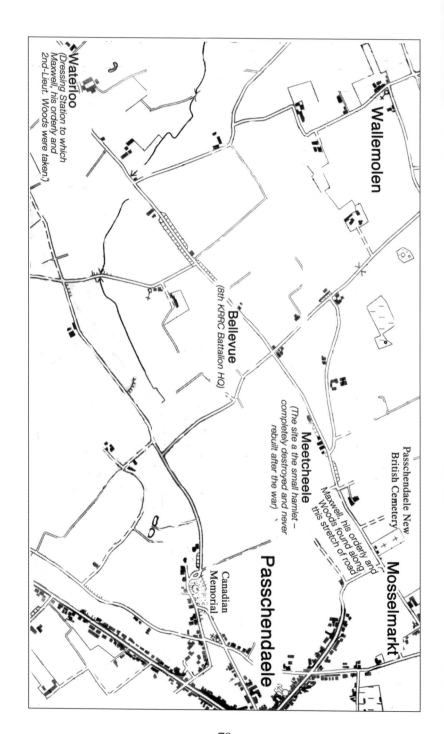

Waterloo
(Dressing Station to which Maxwell, his orderly and 2nd-Lieut. Woods were taken.)

Wallemolen

Bellevue
(8th KRRC Battalion HQ)

Meetcheele
(The site a the small hamlet – completely destroyed and never rebuilt after the war)

Maxwell, his orderly and Woods found along this stretch of road

Passchendaele New British Cemetery

Mosselmarkt

Canadian Memorial

Passchendaele

reconnoître the line, 'about which there was some uncertainty'. The enemy was active with his daily intermittent but regular shelling and disaster struck when all three men were severely wounded, caught by the same exploding shell. They were discovered approximately 200 yards beyond Meetcheele on the road to Mosselmarkt by Brig.-Gen. P. B. C. Skinner, C.M.G., D.S.O.

They were carried to the Waterloo Farm Dressing Station farther back down the road to Gravenstafel. Sadly, Maxwell's orderly and 2nd-Lieut. Woods died on the way there.[4] Maxwell's wound was dressed and he was transported to 101st Field Ambulance Dressing Station in the Ypres Town Prison. There he was to fall unconscious, dying of his wounds in the early hours of the next day, 4 December.

In a letter to Col. Lord Gorell dated 15 December 1917, the Brig.-Gen. explained his finding of the wounded men:

This is how the end came to poor old John, one horrible night. With Prideaux Brune, I was walking up the hellish bit of road from Meetcheele to Mosselmarkt, in our hellish sector, when we came upon John Maxwell, his signalling officer and his orderly, all lying in the road together. The road is so thickly strewn with corpses in that neighbourhood that we would have passed them, only that the man cried out, and I heard John's voice say, 'Is that you, General?' We raised some stretcher bearers, therefore, and had them carried down to the

Canadian graves around a German strongpoint on the Bellevue Spur which was captured on the opening day of the Canadian attack at Passchendaele, 26 October 1917.

Dressing Station, though John was the only one who arrived there alive. They had all been hit by the same shell, and must have been lying in the roadway for some ten minutes before we found them. John was wounded in the lung with a piece of shell, and had, in addition, one leg broken. He was quite conscious, and I stayed with him for a little time at the Dressing Station. His last words to me were, as I went away, 'Good luck to the Brigade, General!'

During the night John wrote a letter to his mother, which he sent to us to post, and from that and what the doctor told me, I had hopes he would recover. He became unconscious during the night, however, and died early in the next morning at the same main Dressing Station. That, briefly, is how I lost the best man and the finest soldier in the Brigade, during a horrible night the events of which I am never likely to forget.

In a letter dated 9 December to Maxwell's mother Skinner wrote:

Of all the officers in the brigade your son is the one whom I could afford to spare least... We, amongst whom your son lived and worked, appreciated his capacity, his conscientiousness and his fearless devotion to duty to the full.

The stretch of road rising to a section of the infamous Meetcheele Ridge just beyond where the hamlet of Meetcheele once stood. This is the road where Lieut.-Col. Maxwell, his orderly and 2nd Lieut. Woods were found by Brig.-Gen. Skinner. The area was studded with German pillboxes and fortified farms. The map reference showing Meetcheele in late 1917 referred to a massive pillbox, the hamlet of that name having been razed to the ground, as with most buildings, hamlets and villages in the Passchendaele sector.

The brigade's Church of England Chaplain, T. W. A. Jones wrote to Maxwell's mother:

His body rests in the burial ground at the prison at Ypres – I went to see the place a short time ago – his spirit is in God's keeping.

In the same letter, Chaplain Jones also recalled an amusing incident. On promoting the idea of a service for the men, Maxwell told chaplain that he would come himself as long as there were some 'decent hymns'. The chaplain offered him the choice of hymns, but instead of choosing three or four, he went through the entire army hymn book dividing all the hymns into three categories: '1st-class hymns', '2nd-class hymns', and 'not-at-any-price hymns'. He chose hymns that 'bucked up the men', ruling out those that were mournful or full of what he called 'sloppy sentiment'. This was the same man who, on duty at Albatross Bank, informed the Chaplain to prepare for burial 50 to 60 bodies lying about in order that they be given a Christian burial and to improve the morale of his own men going up and down the line past them.

Today's complex of buildings on the site of the Waterloo Dressing Station where Maxwell was first treated. One of the many fortified farms in the area, known as Waterloo Farm by many units, it housed a large German strongpoint named, as would be expected, Waterloo.

Jones also spoke of Maxwell's conversations about C Company:

He regarded his company as his family. He got to know every man individually. If any man had any home trouble, he was always sympathetic, he would take endless trouble to write letters and to help.

Of course, everybody, officers, N.C.O.s and men, all regarded your son as a magnificent soldier.

Today, Ypres Reservoir Cemetery is sited on what was an open meadow on the edge of the town known by the Ypres community as 'Plaine d'Amour' before the war: a meadow for lovers and courting couples to spend their time and stroll at leisure. During the war, three cemeteries were started near the prison, the town reservoir and the western gate of the Ypres ramparts. The two between the prison and the reservoir were eventually moved to the third, then called the Cemetery North of the Prison, later named Ypres Reservoir North Cemetery and now, Ypres Reservoir Cemetery.

Standing at John Maxwell's grave in this cemetery gives rise to many thoughts of both the man himself and the great institutions that had moulded his pathway through life. Members of the Officer Training Corps together with the many other pupils of the colleges and public schools of England gave freely of their best in the Great War, Marlborough College, Maxwell's 'local' college, alone lost 749 of its sons boys and men cognisant of duty and sacrifice to the national cause.[5]

The love of country that spurred so many into action in that 'War to end all Wars', is perhaps becoming an outmoded concept in this day and age. Lieut.-Col. John Maxwell D.S.O., M.C., in a letter to a relative, reminds us that a deep love of one's country is a noble, selfless quality that transcends the self:

When the British nation, every jack man, woman, and boy, feels a trickle down its spine at the sound of a bugle, then, and only then, can it – the British nation – begin to think it has a right to win the war. Patriotism doesn't consist in waving a Union Jack and in shouting 'Rule Britannia'. It doesn't even begin there. Patriotism starts at birth. It is a delicate and sensitive plant, highly susceptible to sun on the one hand, and east winds on the other. It grows and develops by careful training and nurturing, until the finished article produces a man who loves his country, symbolised by the King, more than his personal feelings.

It is as a soldier that 'Fighting' or 'Battling' John Maxwell is best remembered. He was a courageous soldier with a gift for leadership, an opinion attested to by his service record.

Personal tributes flooded in after his death, tributes which would have been cautiously received by Maxwell for any sign of false praise which would have been universally dismissed by him as 'eye-wash'.

In death he received perhaps the greatest accolade in a simple statement from Cyniac-Skinner:

I lost the best man and the finest soldier in the Brigade...

There was a feeling amongst the brigade that his 'charmed life' would see him through the war. It was not to be. As a friend put it:

For himself, I have no regret; it is the one he would have chosen.

A well-earned rest for a soldier's hard endeavour is a sentiment reflected in the inscription on his headstone chosen by his mother from Sir Walter Scott's 'Lady of the Lake':

> Soldier rest, thy warfare o'er
> Dream of fighting fields no more.

To stand quietly at his graveside today and contemplate the soldier at rest there is a tangible feeling that this life extinguished in a flash of flame, pain and suffering on a hillside in Flanders was of a calibre that England could ill afford to lose. As Col. Lord Gorell concludes in his reminiscences of the 7th Battalion R.B. 'band of brothers':

To all around him he was more than a beloved leader, more than the noble-hearted friend; he was the embodiment of the first spirit of the New Army, beginning with the day of its birth and continuing, so hope grew, to its day of final victory. It was not to be. The footsteps of Fate followed John through the long months round Ypres, through the Somme, through Arras, to the same scarred soil on which he had fought his first battle, and there at last they overtook him. Where the comrades of the earliest days sleep, there sleeps John... If all the silenced voices could be raised, there would be but one murmur: 'This was the noblest Roman of them all'.

Notes:

1. The Hon, R. Gorell-Barnes went to France with the Brigade as a 2nd-Lieut. in the 7th Rifle Brigade. He became 3rd Baron Gorell on the demise of his brother Maj. the Hon. Henry Gorell-Barnes, 7th London Brigade R.G.A. on 16 January 1917.

2. Capt. The Hon, E. J. Kay-Shuttleworth, Eton and Balliol Scholar, was an officer in the original 7th Rifle Brigade contingent that went on active service in May 1915. He was killed in a motorbike accident in July 1917 in England.

3. Testimony in graves to this period of the battalion's occupation is sparse; many cemeteries in the Ypres Salient had been lost by war's end. A row of riflemen of A Coy., 7th RB in Essex Farm Cemetery in Plot I. Row T. Graves 8-11: 4 men killed from a single shell-burst on a dugout on the canal bank on 13 January 1915.

3a. Amongst Maxwell's personal effects were his pipe and a pouch of tobacco.

4. 2nd-Lieut. Woods, 25th London Regiment (Cyclists) attached 8th King's Royal Rifle Corps is buried in Tyne Cot Cemetery. Plot XVII. Row A. Grave 6.

5. The college Roll of Honour contains the names of 733 Old Boys, 7 Assistant Masters and 9 Staff members. Amongst them are three holders of the Victoria Cross.

Ypres Reservoir Cemetery in the 1920s.

*Only the dead have seen the end of war*
Plato


6

AN AMERICAN AT YPRES

Wainwright Merrill who served as Arthur A. Stanley.


A N EVENING STROLL to the Ypres Reservoir Cemetery as the deepening rays of the sun descend behind the vast edifice of St. Martin's Cathedral, provides today's visitor with an opportunity to spend a few moments of reflection in this busy town. Within the confines of this British cemetery, near the walls of the town prison, is the grave of a young American who enlisted as a Canadian gunner: 19-year old, Wainwright Merrill, who served under the name A. A. Stanley. This American and the hundreds of other young men who lie at their eternal rest following the roar of battle, do so in what was traditionally known by the Ypres community as 'La Plaine d'Amour', an apt name for where the town's young lovers took their ease in days long-gone.

Wainwright Merrill who served as Gunner Arthur A. Stanley, 10th Canadian Siege battery.

The cemetery register confirms that Merrill from Massachussets, U.S.A., changed his name to Arthur A. Stanley upon enlistment in the Canadian Military, the first step in a journey that was to end here, marked by one of the many headstones to be found in military cemeteries of the old Salient.

Details on a headstone provide only simple facts of identity, regiment and date of death of the man who lies beneath it. Sometimes there is a desire to know the full human story behind it, what he looked like, his background, his personality, his hopes and aspirations, and, in this young soldier's case, what internal forces had driven him to leave his comfortable surroundings to travel several thousand miles to serve with a foreign army? These are the impulses that can serve to motivate many a visitor to embark upon a trail of research and discovery following a military cemetery visit.

The brief service of the American divisions in the Salient during the summer of 1918 has an interesting history. After their short period of instruction with the British Second Corps and successful action along the Vierstaat Ridge, the two divisions, the 27th New York State and 30th Tennessee, moved south, ultimately to align themselves with their national army then concentrating. Field Marshal Haig was so impressed with the men from the 'New World' that he fought a political battle to retain them under his command. The two formations took most of their fatal casualties with them to be included in their burial plots, as was their custom. However, here and there around the old Ypres sector they formerly inhabited, like pebbles left on the seashore by the receding tide, a few American graves were left behind and now lie in the sanctuary of the large British cemeteries predominant in the area. Examples of note concern the Americans at Lijssenthoek near Poperinghe: one a sergeant killed by one of the final German long-range heavy calibre artillery shells to be lobbed into the Salient in late October 1918 whilst he directed traffic at the village of Watou. Another vivid reminder of the American presence are the empty plots at Abeele Airfield and Nine Elms cemeteries near Poperinghe. These originally housed the fallen of the 104th Machine Gun Company, 27th (New York) Division and the 30th (Tennessee Division) respectively. When the graves were removed after the war the plots was left empty and never used again.

However, although he would never serve with his own countrymen Merrill was a true native-born American who hailed from Cambridge, on the affluent Eastern Seaboard in Massachussets, the place where George Washington first took command of the rebel Anglo-Americans and turned them into a viable force, thus changing the course of history. His grave is only a few miles from another soldier with a tenuous link to the Revolution, Revere Osler. Buried at Dozinghem Military Cemetery, near Poperinghe[1], Osler was the great-great grandson of Paul Revere, a famous figure from the past whose ride from Lexington Green in 1776 gave the people of Boston the message "The Redcoats are coming" – news that the Red Coat Army of King George III was on the move against them. A move resulting in the famous Battle of Bunker Hill.

Born on the 26 May 1898 to Samuel and Estelle Hatch Merrill, Wainwright had made the Allied cause his own before the entry of the U.S.A. into the war in 1917 by virtue of the fact that he had an English born grandmother on his paternal side. Consequently he developed a deep affinity for all things British, referring to the

Mother Country's struggle as his own. With a public school education and English ancestors he felt a strong empathy with the British cause. This side of his background must have impinged greatly on his character and would shortly prove influential in what was to become the most momentous and fateful decision of his young life.

His educational background had certainly stamped out a bright future for him but, like so many of his fated generation worldwide, if he could have pulled aside the curtain of his own destiny he would surely have been puzzled to discover that all the future had to offer was a muddy grave in a remote part of Europe of which he had little knowledge, called Belgian Flanders. What is more, at the time he would be taking the King's shilling and serving under the flag which his forbears had struggled to cast aside in the colonial days, one hundred and fifty years before. Such are the ironies of life, and death.

He graduated from Cambridge High School during the summer of 1915, progressing to Dartmouth College soon after – his father's 'Alma Mata'. Almost a year later, in 1916, he was selected for Harvard University, in what would have been the class of 1918. He was very happy with the way things were developing in his life and anticipated a fruitful time ahead at Harvard where many of his friends were studying. If destiny had not played its hand there is little doubt his full potential would have been realised.

A broader picture of young Merrill before the war-machine enveloped him can be gained from a post-war memorial volume issued by Harvard detailing those of its sons registered as students who died on the battlefields of Europe. It shows him to be a keen-eyed, resolute young man facing up to what was then an unclouded future. He gazes at the camera seemingly unafraid of what the future might hold.

His planned days at Harvard would certainly be cut short. He was destined never to attain his personal goal of intellectual achievement. At the time of the photograph, circa 1915-16, he could have had no possible awareness of the dramatic events that lay ahead.

The war in Europe was at its horrendous peak and Merrill studied all the news available to him from the various battle fronts with great interest. He became an active member of the Dartmouth Volunteer Training Unit, feeling deep within himself that some form of military training might prove necessary in due course. This realisation gathered pace in his mind whilst, in far-off Picardy, the Somme battles raged, taking an ever increasing toll of combatants of both sides. It seemed inconceivable from the news reports that the British could be sustaining casualties on such a scale. It brought back memories of the American Civil War and the bloodletting on both sides of the Union, a recent memory of only fifty years previously.

The critical manpower situation of the Allies in the autumn of 1916 and the strong urge to assist the country he so admired, led Merrill to take some form of action. In November of that year he crossed the Canadian border under the newly-assumed name of Arthur A. Stanley, and enlisted in the Canadian Field Artillery in Toronto. It is not clear exactly why he changed his name, but under American law he was still considered a minor and he knew his father's consent would not have been forthcoming in the decision he had made. Nothing is known as to whether his father ever made overtures to retrieve his young son from the military but records do show that after five months training at Valcartier Camp, the main instruction depot at the time, he crossed the Atlantic and landed at the port of Liverpool in 1917 just as the grand British-Canadian offensive at Arras began.

One can only wonder at Merrill's thoughts and emotions now that he was in England, the country to whom he had given his allegiance and yet never seen. For several months he underwent further instruction in the aspects of gunnery and by early October of that same year, was ready for war.

On 8 October 1917, just as the Canadian Corps were moving into the Passchendaele front to relieve the exhausted British and Australian troops who had borne the brunt of Third Ypres, Gunner Merrill and his comrades in the 10th Canadian Siege Battery left their training area around Larkhill, Wiltshire and made the sea-crossing to France and from there on to Flanders in order to play their gallant part in the battle. After a period of acclimatisation, the boy from Cambridge moved up into the front line with his battery. What a strange new world must have met his wondering eyes there. It was surely alien to anything they could possibly have imagined as he peered in the early morning light along the Ravebeek Valley near the village of Passchendaele, a sector which the Canadians had recently taken stewardship of. A contemporary account by R.A. Colwell describes the scene:

> Hardly a sign of life for miles and miles. No trees except a few shattered stumps which stood strange in the pale moonlight. No birds sang, no grass to be seen, not even a rat. Mother Nature was as dead as the Canadian bodies seen lying to the front, killed in recent attacks. Only some sticks and stones denoted where a

former farm or homestead had stood. They had been a reality once, because their positions stood out clearly on maps of the area. The earth was churned and rechurned into one muddy mess into which an unsuspecting man could drown if he ventured from the wooden duckboard track. Shell hole broke into shell hole, until they nearly became as one. It was not easy to write of this part of the Salient. Such are the things of which nightmares are made.

This was the 'land of the dead' in which Merrill now found himself. Massachussets, home and family must have seemed another world away. He had brought this change of life-style upon himself through his powerful emotions of loyalty and duty. Tragically, there would be precious little time for him to question his decision. Within a few days, with his battery at the front line, Wainwright Merrill, the boy who had left the safety of a comfortable home, was dead. His war had lasted barely three days. A journey of more than five thousand miles to die in a foreign land.

Wainwright Merrill's headstone at Ypres Reservoir Cemetery. Plot I, Row, Grave 91.

A section of Ypres Reservoir Cemetery as seen from near the Ypres Town prison.

From battery records it seems that the gun pits and crews' billets, in the ruins of an old farm close-by, came under heavy enemy counter-fire at 2 a.m. on the morning of 6 November, 1917 just as the infantry of the Canadian First Division were preparing their final assault on the ruins of Passchendaele, an attack which would prove successful and close down the battle for the winter. Merrill was hit at the height of the enemy barrage. Reports say that he died without regaining consciousness.

The 'great adventure' was over for Wainwright Merrill; his brief time in battle brought to a shattering halt in the mud of a Belgian field. Not quite the patriotic odyssey he had wanted, though his initial decision to come here had been made for all the right reasons. He was not alone in this. Many others had joined him in this bond of brotherhood which so sadly expired on the battlefields of Europe. To his grieving parents, the loss of their youngest son would be a blow from which it would be difficult to recover, but their sorrow  tempered with a tinge of pride for a son who had freely given all a young man had to give.

Wainwright Merrill, like so many of the other casualties of the shelling on that dawn the Canadians secured Passchendaele, was given a temporary grave near the old gun pits on the infamous Bellevue Spur. There it remained until after the Armistice, when peace reigned and all that was left on that barren ridge to show the life of Merrill, was a rudimentary timber cross, muddied and tilting in the howling wind. His comrades had moved on and he was left alone!

The Reservoir Cemetery, one of three on the Plaine d'Amour was taken over from the Belgians in 1915 at the end of Second Ypres. In the early 1920s, the Imperial War Graves Commission developed and concentrated the enclosures with the many graves from outlying districts being brought in to enable the cemetery to achieve its present size of over 2,000 graves, Wainwright Merrill's among them.

To those who best knew him, Merrill displayed the very finest qualities of character at all times. Sensitive to the feelings of others, he would see both sides of an argument and usually give way to avoid hurting the other party. He had that rare quality of being willing and able to carry out his order regardless of any difficulty, a trait that marked him out as a comrade and soldier to be trusted.

His voluntary entry into the Canadian Artillery was typical of his spirit and strength of character. He acknowledged that friends and family might not come to terms with the decision he had taken and yet he felt stronger in himself for having made it. Britain's cause, he had decided, was right and she needed every man she could get to help counter-act the enormous losses she was suffering. Although his own country had not as yet opted to join the fight, the blood within him stirred in a burning desire to assist the 'Old Country'. He and others of his kind had gone forward freely in a common sacrifice and the world could ill-afford to lose them.

Merrill's letters home to his father, brother and various college friends, were published under the title *A College Man in Khaki* in 1920. This details the experiences he underwent and his re-actions to them. In addition, they reflect his strong inner spirit, his belief in opting for a righteous cause and his feelings that it was his privilege to sacrifice everything with a smile to uphold it. A letter written to an old school friend a week before he died gives a clear insight into this spirit:

> Ed, It's a bald sort of fact, just going up into this sector of a particularly infernal hell. It might be hard Ed, leaving everything back there, perhaps for good and all. So, if it should be that old friend I'll say goodbye. But God, how can one say a couple of words and it's all over. You go up the line and try to laugh or smile at least and swallow it down. It's part of the game of course, and it is a noble death we seek out here, out of all the ruck and jetsam of death and broken men and lasting sorrow.
>
> Goodbye Ed.

As if in appeasement to the premonition in this final letter, that 'noble death' he mentioned so bravely was to be his within just a few days.

America lost 115,660 men in the Great War, many of whom, like Merrill, had come, by whatever avenue they could, to the assistance of the Allied cause in advance of their country's entry into the fray in 1917. His modern countrymen come to the European battlefields in ever increasing numbers. Ypres is often on their agenda and a few moments at the Reservoir Cemetery would make a lasting memento of their visit and perhaps 'his' poignant story will encourage others to visit and remember this young American. After all, this is what the former fields of battle and their cemeteries are for... Remembrance, and "If remembered, they can never die."

Notes:

1. 2nd-Lieut. Edward Revere Osler is buried at Dozinghem Military Cemetery, Westvleteren, Belgium, Belgium. Plot IV, Row F, Grave 21.

Charles Sargeant Jagger's Royal Artillery Memorial at Hyde Park Corner, London.

84

*Eyes which, though dimmed with blood or tear,*
*Or the dark shadow itself, see clear.*
G. H. Leonard.

# 7
# SCULPTOR AND SOLDIER
Lieutenant Charles Sargeant Jagger M.C.
2nd Battalion, The Worcestershire Regiment.

CHARLES SARGEANT JAGGER was born in Kilnhurst, Yorkshire on 17 December 1885. He spent his early years as would any other young boy in a small Yorkshire village although it differed in some aspects in that, from a very early age, he showed an interest in becoming a sculptor.

Leaving school at the age of fourteen, he joined the company of Mappin & Webb in Sheffield as a metal engraver, working there for six years, learning his trade before moving to expand his creative talents in 1905 by enrolling as a student at the Sheffield School of Art. In 1907 he won a scholarship to attend the Royal College of Art in London where he further developed his talents and skills rapidly, studying there until 1911 when he decided take up a practice in the art of sculpting, augmenting his earnings by taking the job of a part-time teacher. He was to experience a fair amount of success in his chosen career, gaining many honours and prizes in the world of art, before winning a Rome Scholarship from the Royal College in July 1914, with his *Bacchanalian Group* bronze. This scholarship offered him further opportunity to progress his art, but this was not to be.

War was declared and, in the early September of 1914, forsaking further studies, he renounced his scholarship and enlisted in the Artist Rifles. A year later, in September 1915, he had transferred to the Worcestershire Regiment, holding the rank of 2nd-Lieut.. The 23rd of the month saw him with the 4th Battalion of the regiment, then part of the 88th Infantry Brigade, 29th Division, on a troopship making

2nd Lieut. Charles Sargeant Jagger, 4th Battalion the Worcestershire Regiment in 1915

Jagger's Bacchanalian Group which won him the Prix de Rome

its way to Gallipoli in the Dardenelles. Two months later he was wounded and evacuated back to England to recover. Promoted to Lieutenant, he spent almost two years as a rifle instructor in the Isle of Wight before returning to active service in the November of 1917 with the regiment's 2nd Battalion, this time part of the 100th Infantry Brigade, 33rd Division.

In the March and early April of 1918 the division was in the Ypres Salient taking part in the intermittent fighting on and around the Passchendaele Ridge before moving south into northern France for refit and training. From there it travelled north again, through Bailleul onto Ravelsberg and then into the Army Line reserve trenches running between Neuve Eglise and Romarin in southern Belgium. Here it prepared for serious battle which it knew was coming its way.

German High Command, following its victories on the Somme in March 1918, built on it its successes with speedy conquests in Flanders, and was now intent on breaking the British defences of Ypres, opening the way to the French coast and the Channel Ports, an objective fostered since 1914. Capitalising on the crossing the River Lys west of Armentières, its forces swept up to capture the Messines Ridge, an importnt strategical position lost to its armies the year before, and then moved on to take Mont Kemmel close to the French border, in what was a disastrous week for the Allies.

The British position was desperate. Enemy forces flooded across Flanders toward the French border with the border town of Bailleul taking the brunt of their heavy shellfire. British infantry found itself constantly fighting rearguard actions all along the line in a desperate bid to hold this determined enemy advance.

Neuve Eglise, a small straggling village on the high ground east of Bailleul, lay in the path of the frantic, retreating British force and the seemingly unstoppable advancing German.

This then was the desperate situation in which the division's 100th Brigade now found itself on 12 April 1918. It occupyied the half-completed Army Line reserve trenches covering the approaches to Bailleul with its 2nd Battalion Worcestershire Regiment holding the left of the line and asister battalion, the 16th King's Royal Rifle Corps, positioned on the right.

Lieut. C. S. Jagger, commanding D Company, was responsible for holding the part of the line on the eastern fringes of Neuve Eglise village itself.

Men of these defending battalions watched helplessly as the enemy advanced down the shoulder of the Messines Ridge, setting up their guns in the fields in front of, but out of range of the

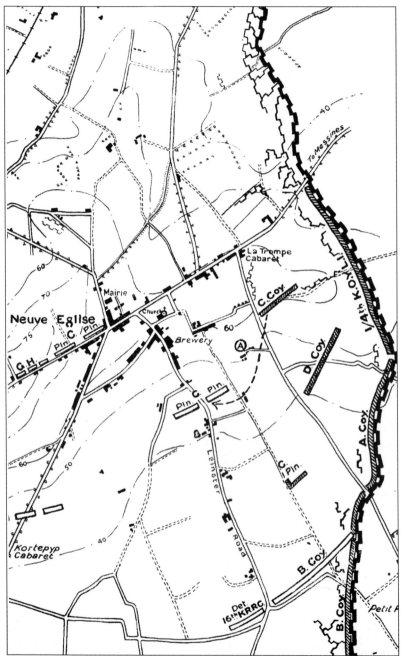

The half-completed Army Line reserve trenches east of Neuve Eglise covering the approaches to Bailleul.

British infantry, and, over open sights, bombarding the village of Neuve Eglise, soon reducing it to heaps of smoking rubble and roofless buildings.

On the morning of the 13th, the enemy massed infantry attacked in force. Companies of the 2nd Worcesters engaged to their front manning a sector of the Army Line trench system, were unaware that another enemy force was advancing to their rear, moving up the Leinster Road from Le Romarin. Having broken through the right of the line, this force was moving closer to the Worcesters' headquarters sited in the local town brewery just south of the church. Anticipating their arrival, Lieut.-Col. Stoney, the Worcesters' commanding officer, ordered every available man out the headquarters to the crossroads west of the church to hold back the advance. He then ordered his C Company to move at once to counter attack. The company moved in from its position east of the village and closed in on the rear of the enemy in Leinster Road, catching them in a sunken road, where fire from the crossroads and C Company itself took its heavy toll on them. Although putting up a fierce resistance the Germans, penned in the sunken road with no means of escape, lost some 60 men killed

The ruined brewery just south of Neuve Eglise Church – once the 2nd Worcestershire's Battalion Headquarters in the village.

before the remaining 20-odd surrendered. Amongst the German dead heaped in the road, the Worcesters gathered for themselves 6 light machine-guns.

Nevertheless the Worcesters' position was untenable and at 2.00 pm Stoney gave instructions to withdraw his companies in the Army Line to the outskirts of the village itself. Constant enemy attacks throughout the afternoon delayed these orders reaching his Army Line companies until 6.00 pm that evening.

Now the Worcesters found themselves cut-off on both flanks, with no support or communication to their rear. Vicious hand-to-hand street fighting was taking place in the village, the streets in and around the ruins being packed with troops of both sides. This was particularly so in front of the church and in the village square housing its *Mairie*. The Worcesters' headquarters was again under threat and this time its garrison was forced to remove itself and take up a new position in the local Hospice north of the village on the Dranoutre road.

The three forward companies of the Worcesters had fallen back as ordered after dark on 13 April. Under constant pressure, they organised their defences a little nearer to the village. They were all

The site of the brewery just south of Neuve Eglise Church – once the 2nd Worcestershire's battalion headquarters in the village.

battle weary and exhausted, and their supply of ammunition was running dangerously low. Eventually the pressure became too much to take and most of the British troops were forced to surrender. But many individual parties managed to fight their way through the village, finding their way to join what was left of the battalion at the Hospice.

On the left flank, Lieut. Jagger commanding the remnants of his D Company, showed talents of a type different to those of his vocation for sculpture. He organised his men into defensive positions, holding back repeated enemy attacks until they were virtually out of ammunition. He then implemented an orderly retreat, with small groups of the troops moving independently to the buildings of La Tromphe Cabaret on the crest of the Messines–Neuve Eglise road between the second line of defence west of the Army Line and the entrance to Neuve Eglise itself. Retreating stragglers from other units joined his depleted company and, making full use of them, he again organised and consolidated the defence at this point until reinforcements arrived. While disengaging and withdrawing his detachment to

The building on the site of La Tromphe Cabaret today – Lieut. Jagger set up a last line of defence here before he was wounded.

cover and to rest a while before rejoining the battalion at the Hospice, he was severely wounded. He was awarded the Military Cross for his work during this action.

Having now set up their new defences and battalion headquarters within and in front of the Hospice, the 2nd Worcesters were to suffer sustained attack throughout the whole evening, Dawn of the 14th saw them completely surrounded and taking heavy trench mortar bombardment and machine-gun fire from three sides. Gradually the German pressure forced the British line back astride the Wulverghem road. The village square and the Hospice north of it, now housing the Worcesters' battalion headquarters, became the front line.

The Worcesters held their own, fighting desperately, beating off frequent attacks by enemy riflemen, but persistent machine-gun fire, mortar bombs and constant artillery fire was causing them heavy casualties. About 11 am, Assistant-Adjutant Capt. J. Crowe led a sortie against two enemy machine-guns which were sited on the high ground west of the Hospice.[1] This action proved successful, effectively eliminating the two machine-gun crews,

The Hospice, pre 1914. In April 1918 the 2nd Worcestershires retreated to this building and set up its headquarters therein.

and easing some of the pressure on the defenders in the Hospice. Capt. Crowe and his party held the ground until, at 1.45 pm, Lieut.-Col. Stoney, gave the order to retire and the exhausted and battle-weary Worcesters, 20 to 30 of them wounded, left the partly ruined Hospice, making their way onto the Dranoutre road and up to the safety of the village of Locre near Kemmel.

The action at Neuve Eglise ended Lieut. Charles Jagger's active service. Still suffering from his wounds after the Armistice, he returned to civilian life and his beloved sculpting, but he was to be forever haunted by his wartime experiences in both Gallipoli and on the Western Front. He led a very active and busy life, producing sculptures from commissions all over the world.[3]

By their size and form alone, his works on the subject of conflict starkly presented the grim and intimidating realities of man at war. These all reflect his early training and education, coupled with his frightening experiences in those two theatres of war in which he served, fought and suffered severe wounds.[2]

A realist he was. There was certainly nothing vague about his sculptures. Working with stone and bronze, he dealt with facts in a distinctive and sensitive way.

He was elected an Associate of the Royal Academy in 1916 and the same year he was awarded a Special Gold Medal for the most outstanding work.

He was to die of a heart attack in 1934 at the age of 48. A short life, with much achieved and a multitude of works to remind all who see them of his uncanny ability to capture, with vigour, the aggression, determination and strength of man's spirit when forced into violent circumstances.

Notes.

1 Assistant-Adjutant Capt. J. Crowe was awarded the Victoria Cross and 2nd-Lieut. Pointon the Military Cross for this exploit.

2. Responsible for many works on the subject of men at war, Jagger himself considered his bronze 'No Man's Land' in the Tate Gallery as his finest work, although many would give that credit to his Royal Artillery Memorial at Hyde Park Corner, London.

3. He worked on many subjects other than that of war. His statue of King George V stands in Delhi; he was commissioned to sculpt H. R. H. the Prince of Wales (later King Edward VIII) by the Viscount Esher; his 'Christ the King' is on the façade of Liverpool's Roman Catholic Cathedral; his 'Scandal' executed for Lord Melchet can be seen at Mulberry House; 'The Mocking Birds' was commissioned by Freda Lady Forres etc. These and many other works give credence to his talent, and particularly so the grim, expressive, inherently strong presentations of the ordinary soldier.

O LITTLE MIGHTY BAND THAT STOOD FOR ENGLAND THAT WITH YOUR BODIES FOR A LIVING SHIELD GUARDED HER SLOW AWAKING

NO MAN'S LAND
Jagger considered his bronze 'No Man's Land' commissioned by the British School in Rome, as his finest work.

94

THE SENTRY
Small bronze produced for Messrs Watts,
Manchester.

Small bronze produced for the Memorial to
the men of the Great Western Railway,
Paddington Station, London.

THE DRIVER
The model for 'The Driver' on the Royal Artillery Memorial.

RECUMBENT FIGURE
North face, Royal Artillery Memorial.

Charles Sargeant Jagger, sculptor, working on his Royal Artillery Memorial.

**Lieutenant Ronald W Poulton Palmer**
1/4th Battalion, the Royal Berkshire Regiment.
England and Harlequins Rugby Club.

**Lieutenant Frederick H Turner**
10th (Scottish) Battalion,
the King's (Liverpool Regiment).
Scotland and Liverpool Rugby Club.

*And its not for the sake of a ribboned coat,*
*Or the selfish hope of a season's fame,*
*But his Captain's hand on his shoulder smote -*
*'Play up! play up! and play the game!'*
Sir Henry Newbolt: Vitai Lampada


# 8
# CAPTAINS VALIANT
Ronald William Poulton Palmer and Frederick Harding Turner
Belgian Flanders, 1915.

WHEN ENGLAND PLAYED SCOTLAND at rugby at Inverleith in March 1914, few among the thousands watching an English 16–15 victory could have imagined that war was about to descend on Europe and that for 5 years the battlefield would be taking precedent over the sporting arena. Of the 30 players on the field that day, just over a third were destined to give their lives before the 1918 Armistice. They included both national team captains, Ronald Poulton Palmer of England and Harlequins and Frederick Harding Turner of Scotland and Liverpool. Within just 14 months of the match, both would lay in soldiers' graves in Flanders, barely more than a mile or two apart. Such is one of war's ironies.

Traditionally England and Scotland, the old, bitter enemies of bye-gone days, have pitched their strength and matched each other's valour on the battlefields of history, Bannockburn, Culloden and Preston spans part of their joint story. A sound alliance since the union of the two countries has nevertheless maintained a good-natured rivalry for the past 100 years or more, Once the roar of battle had subsided over the centuries, competition of a different kind endured between both nations on the sports field. Not quite the blood-letting of past history but nonetheless frenetic and highly competitive. Anyone doubting the intensity of this modern competition need look no further than Murrayfield or Twickenham on the day of an international rugby match to see that sport has now superseded battle for the roaring tribes. Sporting heroes sprang up to replace the former warriors, men in whom others would, and could, find inspiration and leadership. This notwithstanding, Scotland and its martial spirit has always been a major recruiting ground for the British Army, with the Royal Scots Regiment alone providing more battalions and heroes than most - a perfect example of this unique bond between two countries.

On the rugby field Ronald William Poulton Palmer, Oxford University, Harlequins and Liverpool Rugby Clubs, developed qualities that saw him progress toward the captaincy of the English team in 1914 having played for his country 17 times. He had already made his name in the game by setting a record in 1909 when scoring five tries in the Oxford versus Cambridge 'Varsity' match and was one of the very few players who won an international cap before they had been awarded their Blue at Oxford University.

North of the English/Scottish border, his good friend Frederick Harding Turner, Oxford University, Saracens and Liverpool Rugby Clubs, became a name to inspire his fellow-Scots. Graced with the nickname 'Tanky', he became captain of the Scottish national rugby team. Strange how both Ronald Poulton Palmer's and Frederick 'Tanky' Turner's educational and sporting paths followed the same course, eventually becoming Rugby Football captains of their respective countries: Poulton Palmer, traditionally of the 'old school' and a most graceful player and leader, whilst Turner, as his nickname 'Tanky' implied, led the Scottish with power and aggression.

Born at Reading, Berkshire in 1887, Ronald Poulton was, through his mother, a member of the Palmer family of the Huntley & Palmer biscuit company. He changed his name to Poulton Palmer when he claimed his inheritance and became a member of the board of directors of the company through the death of his uncle, but chose not to use the 'Poulton Palmer' surname. Even though his emergence from this affluent background gave him a comfortable existence, it did not prevent him from applying his verve and industry, as displayed on the rugby field, to assisting less-fortunate boys from poorer parts of the town in sporting and social activities in order to help them achieve a better standard of life. Had he lived there can be little doubt that Poulton Palmer, as a social reformer, would have contributed much to his community, his name synonymous with philanthropy in his Berkshire habitat. The centenary history of Oxford University's Rugby Club says his good looks, 'purity of character' and extraordinary combination of talents' made him a much loved man.

Frederick "Tanky' Turner was, by all accounts, a more rugged and forthright individual who could be relied upon both as a friend and mentor of those placed beneath him. Born in Liverpool of Scottish parents on 29 May 1888, he was educated at Sedburgh School, Yorkshire, and Trinity College Oxford where he gained his love of sports. The two rugby players first met at Oxford University in 1909 when Turner was a member of the University Rugby Club committee and Poulton Palmer was a possible candidate for joining the team. They played together against Cambridge in the annual 'Varsity' matches until leaving university to take up their respective working careers. In 1913, having moved to Manchester to gain experience in the family business, Poulton Palmer was to enjoy the company of 'Tanky" Turner on the rugby field again when he joined Liverpool Rugby Club to play under the captaincy of his old friend.

In August 1914, Poulton Palmer progressed to the military system as a Lieutenant with the 1/4th Battalion, the Royal Berkshire Regiment. The battalion formed part of the new 48th Midland Division and left England for France in March 1915. Turner, already a Territorial soldier, had joined the Liverpool Scottish as a 2nd-Lieut. in the May of 1912, Promoted Lieutenant in October, 1914 he left for the front on 2 November with the 10th (Scottish) Battalion, the King's (Liverpool Regiment) TF, better known as the Liverpool Scottish. It was the first Territorial battalion of the regiment to leave England,

On 25 November the 10th King's, joined the 9th Brigade, 3rd Division, II Corps, then in reserve at Westoutre in Belgian Flanders. On the 27th, the brigade was billeted in the small village of Locre close to Kemmel and moved into the front line to the east of Mount Kemmel, the large eminence that dominated this part of the country.

'Tanky' Turner was a close friend of a fellow officer who was to enter the annals of British military history as one of only three men to be awarded the Victoria Cross and bar. Such a man was the medical officer of the 10th King's Liverpools. Lieut. Noel Godfrey Chavasse, later M.C., V.C. and Bar, son of the Bishop of Liverpool. He was severely wounded at St. Julien in 1917 and never recovered. He died peacefully in his sleep at the dressing station to which he was carried, and now lies in Brandhoek New Military Cemetery, Vlamertinghe just west of Ypres.

Standing at the Kemmel crossroads it is easy to imagine the activities of these soldier friends – Lieut. Noel Chavasse working at the Regimental Aid Station, and his friend and fellow Lieut. 'Tanky' Turner, a company officer, discharging his duties at the Battalion Headquarters. Both the Aid Station and the Headquarters were sited along the La Clytte road west of the crossroads, near Rossignol Wood, a place referred to by writer and poet Edmund Blunden as "full of the songs of the nightingale".

The pharmacy that stands on the site of a Regimental Aid Post...

... and the restaurant on the site of The King's (Liverpool Regiment) Headquarters

Both sites are easily identified today, the local pharmacy with its green cross insignia being that of the old Regimental Aid Post and the restaurant, further along the road to its right, that of the King's Headquarters. It is not hard to imagine the feverish activity that surrounded both places in the dark and mud of a Flemish night – stretcher-bearers carrying the wounded to dressing station to be left for the spirited help to be given them by Noel Chavasse and his team of helpers, and the flurry of runners and other personnel entering and leaving, and generally crowding the entrance to Battalion Headquarters of the 10th King's.

Four months later, Ronald Poulton Palmer, having followed his sporting friend and opponent to Flanders with the 1/4th Royal Berkshire Regiment, was billeted in Romarin, a hamlet in southern Belgium 2 miles east of the village of Ploegsteert close to the Franco/Belgian border. Based here, its troops were involved in digging defence trenches and generally fortifying the line around La Plus Douve Farm on the eastern bank of the River Douve, north of the Bois de Le Gheer, or 'Plugstreet Wood' as it was known to them. The battalion then moved into rest billets at the crossroads on the Estaires road south of Steenwerk in northern France. On 15 April it was moved again to the Ploegsteert area to relieve a battalion of the Hampshire Regiment in Plugstreet Wood itself. Here it was employed in developing reserve and support breastwork defence systems in and around the wood, a supposedly 'quiet' sector of the line. Palmer with D Company of the regiment, found himself second in command while on trench duty and specifically in command of all work in the trench line systems. On the 17th of the month the battalion moved into the line north of the wood taking over the trenches south of the River Douve. Now billeted in the Ploegsteert village schoolhouse, Poulton Palmer and his working parties began a programme of defence repair and strengthening in the trench 30 and 40 sections of the line to the left and right of Anton's Farm, a British strongpoint/observation post and dugout complex north of Prowse Point.

Given the opportunity, both friends and former national rugby captains, might well have been amused to know that they had both served in Flanders, no more than a good sprint apart, but that was not to be.

It was Turner to whom fate dealt the first blow. The 10th King's since its arrival in Belgium, had been continually fighting both the elements of its first winter in the line and an ever aggressive and active enemy. On 8 January the sorely depleted battalion left its

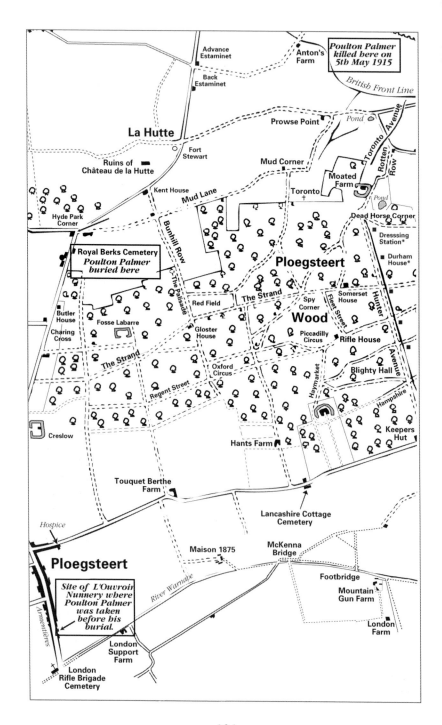

Poulton Palmer
killed here on
5th May 1915

British Front Line

Advance
Estaminet

Anton's
Farm

Back
Estaminet

La Hutte

Prowse Point

Pond

Toronto Avenue

Rotten Row

Fort
Stewart

Ruins of
Château de la Hutte

Mud Corner

Moated
Farm

Kent House

Mud Lane

Toronto

Pond

Hyde Park
Corner

Bunhill Row

Dead Horse Corner

Dressing
Station*

Royal Berks Cemetery
Poulton Palmer
buried here

The Palisade

Ploegsteert

Durham
House*

Red Field

The Strand

Spy
Corner

Somerset
House

Fleet Street

Hunter Avenue

Butler
House

Fosse Labarre

Gloster
House

Wood

Piccadilly
Circus

Rifle House

Charing
Cross

The Strand

Oxford
Circus

Regent Street

Haymarket

Blighty Hall

Hampshire

Creslow

Hants Farm

Keepers
Hut

Touquet Berthe
Farm

Lancashire Cottage
Cemetery

Hospice

Maison 1875

McKenna
Bridge

Footbridge

Ploegsteert

Site of L'Ouvroir
Nunnery where
Poulton Palmer
was taken
before his
burial.

River Warnave

Mountain
Gun Farm

London
Farm

Armentières

London
Support
Farm

London
Rifle Brigade
Cemetery

billets in Locre and marched with the 9th Brigade to Kemmel where they relieved the 7th Brigade in the line. They took over the front trenches and again were to find themselves in constant action, experiencing frequent artillery duels and ever-increasing sniper activity. On 10 January, barely two months after arriving in the area, Lieut. 'Tanky' Turner was sniped whilst on duty in the trench line and died immediately. Stretcher-bearers called out to collect his body were accompanied by his good friend Noel Chavasse. They carried him almost 3 kilometres to be buried in a small plot in the village of Kemmel's churchyard. Today this small plot rests quietly amongst the civilian graves, separate from the churchyard's larger British military cemetery enclosure which was concentrated after the war from local graves found in the district. Such was the reputation of Lieut. 'Tanky' Turner that, when his elder brother William, having recently received his commission in the Reserve Battalion of the 10th King's, was posted to the front on 18 January, a special petition put forward by the men saw him attached to the platoon with which his brother was so popular. He was promoted Lieutenant in May 1915. Like his brother he was a keen sportsman. He was killed in action at 32-years old while leading his men in the advance on Bellewaarde Farm in June 1915. They had just charged and captured a trench when a heavy shell burst close by, killing him instantly. His name is commemorated on the Menin Gate at Ypres.

Lying alongside 'Tanky' Turner in Kemmel churchyard is another famous sportsman of the 10th Liverpool Scottish. On 25 January, 1915, two weeks after his fellow officer Turner died, 36-year old Lieut. Percy Dale Kendall, an English rugby international himself, was sniped and killed in the same area as Turner. The graves of both Lieutenants were lost in later shelling of the area, today confirmed by their memorial headstones being inscribed: 'Believed to be'.

At 12.15 am on the night of 4-5 May 1915, Poulton Palmer, supervising a working party strengthening the Anton's Farm trench systems, was sniped and killed, the first officer in the battalion to fall. His body was carried to the L'Ouvroir des Soeurs de Charité, a nunnery south of Ploegsteert village on the Le Bizet road. The next evening he was buried in the 1/4th Berkshire's plot at Hyde Park Corner at the western edge of Plugstreet Wood. The burial ceremony was conducted by the Reverend Michael Bolton Furse, Bishop of Pretoria, then visiting the battlefields and, by chance, a close friend of Poulton Palmer's family. In a letter to Raymond's family, the Bishop wrote:

We buried him yesterday evening in a wood where everything told us of the resurrection and a new life, in the glorious outburst of a new spring : it was a beautiful service, so simple and so real. Just his company, his brother officers and a few others who could get away.

His commanding officer wrote to the family:

When I went round his old company as they stood to at dawn, almost every man was crying.

Lieut. Challoner, a fellow-officer and close friend in the 1/4th Berkshires was to write:

After the service, the company presented arms, and the officers saluted individually and said a little prayer for the dear fellow.

The small enclosure in Kemmel churchyard with the headstones of Lieut. F. 'Tanky' Turner, fellow rugby player, Lieut. P. D. Kendall and that of an unknown soldier.

Tributes to the family flowed for the man who had written after the death of his peacetime friend and international rugby football rival, 'Tanky' Turner:

... I have played behind many packs of forwards, but never have I been so freed from anxiety as when those forwards were led by Fred Turner. His play, like his tackle, was hard and straight and never have I seen him the slightest bit perturbed or excited and in this fact lay the secret of his great power of control.

Rugby captains and lieutenants Ronald Poulton Palmer and Frederick 'Tanky' Turner lie at rest as close to each other in death as their sporting exploits had dictated in life. One at Kemmel the other at Ploegsteert.

Lieut. Billy Grenfell, soldier poet, who also fell in 1915, provides an insight of death on the battlefield most fitting for two valiant captains:

*Death is such a frail barrier out here,*
*men cross it smilingly and gallantly each day.*

Lieut. Poulton Palmer's original grave marker at the Hyde Park Corner (Royal Berks) Cemetery on the western fringe of Ploegsteert Wood, 1915.

Poulton Palmer's grave marker today (a CWGC replacement to the original which was destroyed during the war) inset into the eastern wall of Holywell Cemetery, Oxford.

GV RI

Dieu et mon Droit

HE whom this scroll commemorates was numbered among those who, at the call of King and Country, left all that was dear to them, endured hardness, faced danger, and finally passed out of the sight of men by the path of duty and self-sacrifice, giving up their own lives that others might live in freedom.

Let those who come after see to it that his name be not forgotten.

*L/Cpl. A.R.M. Stewart*
*17th . Bn. A.I.F.*

*For a moment in time He passed this way,*
*Then with the briefest of smiles, He had gone his way*
Tony Spagnoly

# 9
# IN SEARCH OF ALF STEWART
## 17th Battalion (8th Reinforcement) A.I.F.
### Belgian Battery Corner, Ypres.

J UST BEFORE CHRISTMAS 1915, the 17th Battalion (8th Reinforcement) A.I.F. mostly men from New South Wales, left Sydney, Australia on the troopship *HMAT (A60) The Aeneas* bound for Egypt. The battalion, around 1200 men, had generally been recruited from the same area, went through their basic training together, and were now set on the high seas for the next part of life's great adventure.

The Gallipoli operation had been concluded with the silent evacuation from the Peninsula. Leaving their fallen behind the Australian strength was now being bolstered in the desert near Cairo to be ready for the next operation for which the General Staff would require them.

Rifleman Alfred Robert Morison
Stewart 17th Battalion A.I.F.

Among their number was a young rifleman named Alfred Robert Morison Stewart, a single man of 25 years from Kogarah near Sydney. Stewart was a quiet lad who hailed from a large family of proud Scottish roots and heritage. Like so many of his generation both in Australia, and back in the mother country, a rocklike Christian tradition seemed to be the cement which held the family unit together. Bible readings, hymn singing, and regular church attendance appeared to be the order of the day. This is a thread which was plain to perceive in all his letters written from abroad back to the family. These young men left Australia imbued with the spirit to serve and fight for 'King and Country' – the 'Mother Country' as Britain was romantically viewed at the turn of the 20th century. Britain was a place most of them had never seen, and their opinions of her would change dramatically as war dragged on, and the horrendous casualty took toll of their numbers.

Many viewing the Sydney Heads in the wake of *The Aeneas* as she hit the southern oceans on that morning of 20 December 1915 were fated never to see their homeland again. Alfred Robert Morison Stewart, Regimental No 3622 would be among this poignant roster.

For the moment though on his first venture from home, a general excitement took over as he watched the protective naval vessels weaving in and out of the ships. Perhaps he was thinking of his friends still back in Kogarah at the printing firm where he had worked as a trainee letterpress operator. Not everyone was in the forces.

When the troops landed at Port Cairo, the place was a hive of Australian bustle and activity but his first visit to the Pyramids on 12 February 1916 with friends, left him strangely unmoved at one of the wonders of the ancient world. He observed blandly:

A wonderful structure, but no real architecture – just one stone on top of the other

As the summer of 1916 drew on, the war in Europe began to increase in intensity as the Australians gained experience in the new conditions. Instruction in trench warfare took place between Armentières and Fleurbaix whilst the ghastly experience of the 5th Australian Division at Fromelles was a reminder that the enemy was of a calibre similar to the one they fought against in Gallipoli.

Alf and the 17th Battalion weren't involved in this action but, as the time of their involvement in the 'mincing machine' of Pozières drew near, they were paraded at Warloy Baillon, west of Albert (home of one of the main machine-gun schools) and marched past General Birdwood – who saluted them and passed comment on their soldierly bearing. Now a Lance-Corporal, Alf seemed to think this gesture did wonders for the morale of the men.

When eventually in the front line near Pozières the battalion was to endure terrible bombardments and Alf was confronted with the realities of war when two of his friends were killed alongside him and:

... I was knocked over three times from the concussion of shells bursting near me, but thank God I was spared.

His baptism of fire was complete, but his spiritual strength never deserted him and his bible was a constant companion in the trenches.

On 29 July 1916, again under severe shelling:

I felt down in the dumps and for comforts sake I read my dear Ma's favourite chapter, John 14. It took me out of myself for a while.

During those terrible bombardments Alf would always find comfort in prayer 'But the nerve strain is awful'. When these bouts of shelling ended around that pulverised village of Pozières, Alf and his mates were always 'Tired but shaken'.

A premature explosion took place on the 3 August whilst he and a friend were taking a look at the 'huge mine crater' (probably 'Y Sap') when a fragment of a shell's copper band embedded in his little finger, but the doctor said he would only bandage the wound up and extract the fragment when things eased off.

Life was a constant source of worry in the trenches just living and surviving the constant enemy retaliatory barrages, but his luck ran out a few days later on the 5 August.

The battalion had been in the thick of the ferocious close combat fighting and shelling associated with the tactically vital village of Pozières and the high ground around the old windmill site, the site of today's memorial to the 2nd Australian Division. The destiny of war caught up with Alf on the 5th whilst the battalion were engaged near Munster Alley, a sector where close range bombing activities were always particularly vicious.

Fritz had some balloons up and we were in full view of them, and he started shelling us with shrapnel. I felt, oh I'm blowed if I will keep ducking. After we got our spades and shovels out and were moving off, a couple of shrapnel shells came dangerously close. I was at the end of the file. One huge shrap' shell came howling up the valley, and a second after I felt as if someone had hit me on my right arm with a red hot poker. There was an immediate metallic clang with the burst and I knew I had been hit. I stumbled a bit, and Mr C called out, but I said it's alright, it's only my arm, so I threw down my rifle and spade for the others and walked down to the dressing station towards Albert.

A 'Digger' visiting his mate's grave on the overgrown Pozières battlefield.

Although Alf made light of it, his wound was serious enough to warrant his being transferred to a base hospital for more intensive treatment and subsequently to an enforced period of care, rest and recuperation back in England.

His first glimpse of the 'old country', which he had hardly expected to see, was quite an exciting experience for him, and he was very impressed with the neat farms and the various colours of green in the fields he saw from the train. The welcome he and the other wounded Australians received from the English was impressive and Alf felt it helped his recovery. He wrote many letters on his experiences in England to his family in Kogarah. In the hospital in Oxford, he found it quite a 'comforting' touch that the number of his bed in the ward, in the basement of a drill hall, was 17 – the same as his battalion. He liked that link.

While regaining his strength and the use of his injured arm, Alf was able to immerse himself in the atmosphere and historic presence of Oxford, visiting as many 'tourist' sites as he could, delighting in the sounds and sights. He frequently visited London to see places he thought he could never possibly see, places he had often read about – Buckingham Palace with the royal standard blowing in the wind, Trafalgar Square, Piccadilly Circus, the Strand, Aldgate, Old Street, The Bank, Petticoat Lane, the city places so well renowned and the lights ablaze in the shops. He experienced the Zeppelin air raid warnings and had the dubious pleasure of being taken to see the remains of one which had been shot down. This visit, together with the frequent Zeppelin alerts, made him aware of the fact that the civilian population of Britain was now as much in the front line as he and his friends had been. He wrote home about this, all very illuminating to a lad fresh from the outback 'down under'. His letters are packed with detail of the sights, the streets and all those things that impressed him and which all seemed a far cry from his native Kogarah. That was another world away.

He travelled north to Edinburgh feeling the inherent native pride of a Scotsman arise in him. There his many cousins looked after him in royal fashion, whilst he delighted in seeing the house where his father had been born, the school he went to and even a couple of elderly men who remembered him at school. Again he spent as much of his time there visiting the many sights as he could – and writing home about them. The Western Front and all the depressing news generated by it seemed to be another world.

He felt a strange affinity with Scotland, the 'land of his roots' but in November 1916 he was obliged to leave his cousins, and the welcomes he had received from them, and move south to the Salisbury Plain on reduced duty to regain full fitness with other Australian wounded before going to France to fill the depleted ranks caused by the ever lengthening casualty list. Alf viewed this prospect with an inner trepidation, but he knew his division had been involved in some major actions since his departure from Pozières, and he wanted to be a part of the unique 'bonding' the battalion could give him, and play his part – that was what he volunteered for. The awful experiences on the Somme battlefield had not weakened this resolve.

He was not long at the holding camp at Wilton near Salisbury before he was marked fit for active service and scheduled to leave for France on 16 November 1916 with other Australian reinforcements bound for Boulogne. Before he left, however, he and friends were able to visit that mysterious site of so much interest, Stonehenge. Writing home, he pondered the whys and wherefores of this mighty edifice and could not see it as a place of worship for the ancient druids. How had those massive stones been transported to the site? How were they placed in such a precise way?, These questions stayed with him until his eventual arrival in France where his mind was refocused was once more on the demanding routine of daily drills and retraining demanded of him for several weeks in the infamous Bull Ring at Etaples near Boulogne.

His time here was miserable as 'every day at the ring it seemed to either drizzle or snow'. He found it a good 'test' for his injured arm, but he viewed it all stoically. The one thing that gave him great pleasure there was meeting up with several close friends amongst the other recovered wounded from his old company in the 17th Battalion. The prospect of them rejoining the battalion and going back to the front together pleased Alf, offering a little light to an otherwise dark future. On New Year's Eve 1916, just before he left the Bullring, he was in contemplative mood when he wrote:

Thank God for sparing me so far, when this date comes round again, I hope I will have been able to contribute to a good cause.

That New Year's Eve was the last that for Alf Stewart would see.

When he rejoined his battalion, he found they had been engaged in a war of decisive movement. The enemy had conducted an organised retirement to its new defensive position along the Hindenburg Line which lay to the north of Bapaume, so he was back in the Somme area again. The general destruction and desecration of the hitherto untouched countryside by the retiring enemy, did not meet with Alf's orderly mind, and found a disfavour with him in his letters home. He realised he was not far from where he had been injured eight months before, so he and some friends:

... went for a walk over the old ground. From the great La Boiselle crater to near the end of Shrapnel Gulley. We saw the graves of Capt. Chambers and Tom Marion. I took a snap of the place where I was hit, and of the wooden memorial to the men of the 17th Battalion who fell at Pozières between 25th July–5th August 1916. They are glad because they are at rest.

As they followed up the enemy retreat, they saw the beautiful orchards and kitchen gardens ruthlessly destroyed, and it made the 'Australian blood boil'. A very needless and wickedly wanton destruction as they saw it.

In 1917 the war moved up a gear and the 2nd Division found itself inexorably drawn into the cauldron of what became the misty region of Flanders, or as one old veteran dryly observed, 'If you ain't wet, it ain't Flanders'. The expertly executed attack on the Messines Ridge, on 7 June, the opening of Field Marshal Haig' Flanders Offensive, had been outstandingly successful through the perfect fusion of sound planning, deep dug mines, sweeping artillery bombardment and well coordinated air and infantry tactics. Now in high summer, after a good opening to the Passchendaele Offensive on 31 July, German resistance stiffened and then that age-old ally to the German army, stormy weather, turned the battlefields into a slimy morass.

The Australian Corps was held back until the September action,

An artist's impression of the raising of the Australian flag on the Anzac blockhouse by troops of the Australian 2nd Division on 20 September 1917.

the beginning of the Battle of the Menin Road, when the fortified woodland of Polygon Wood became the prime objective.

The defining moment of the first Anzac onslaught came at dawn on the 20 September when in a light rain, the 2nd Division storm troops raised the Australian flag over the two-tiered concrete command post marked on maps of the time as 'Anzac'. This powerful feature marked the crest of the slight upland rise of the same name that commanded the northern edge of Polygon Wood and its approaches to the village of Zonnebeke. The blockhouse was built into the ruins of a small farm. The rebuilt farm still marks the site today.

Success at this tactically vital position would allow the follow up Anzac division, the 5th, to continue the advance and secure the wood totally. Their divisional memorial perpetuates the victory today.

The 17th and its sister 18th Battalion, mostly lads from New South Wales played an important part in this historic action, and their casualties littered the ground around the pillbox, and the gentle ridge on which it stood.

One of the men badly hit here was Alf Stewart, and sadly it seemed his 14,000 mile journey from far off Kogarah to do his duty in a cause he fervently believed in, neared its finale. Survivors after the action stated:

Alf went forward to aid Sgt. Watson lying wounded in No Mans Land.

The Anzac blockhouse atop the Anzac Ridge in Zonnebeke. Once a major German strongpoint, after 20 September, a leaning point for Aussie rifles.

He volunteered with no thought for his own safety. Scything machine-gun fire wounded him in both legs.

Both men were picked up by the company stretcher bearers, and taken to the Main Dressing Station on the Menin Road in the direction of Ypres. As they went along, a shell landed close by them, and this time the badly injured Alf Stewart was mortally wounded.

By the normal process of casualty evacuation Alf's wounds were dressed and he was being transported back to the Casualty Clearing Stations farther behind the lines, when he obviously needed further treatment or he passed away on route causing him to be left at the small dressing station at Belgian Battery Corner on the Dickebusch Road just west of Ypres. Whatever the case, the lad from Kogarah was finally laid to rest in the little plot beside the dressing station with others from his battalion who fell on that day.

His grave today lies among 480 British and Empire fallen, and his message epitaph proclaims:

*He being dead yet speaketh*
*... and he does down through the years.*

His odyssey was over.

Today, the farm on the crest of the old Anzac Ridge at Zonnebeke marks the spot where the German Anzac blockhouse stood.

Belgian Battery Corner Cemetery was started by the 8th Division to accommodate the influx of casualties from 3rd Ypres fighting, and named after the Belgian unit of heavy guns '1st Groupe Provisoire Regt D'Artillerie' who were based here in 1915.

The Belgian Battery Corner Dressing Station in 1917

L/Cpl. Alf Stewart's
original grave marker

There is a postscript to this story.

A couple of years ago Mr Bob McAlpine in New South Wales, Australia, called to tell the story of his great uncle Alfred Stewart, saying that no one from the family had ever visited the grave, nor had they seen a photograph of it other that an early regimental marker.

As it is so simple these days to determine the site of a serviceman's grave in the old Salient, a visit of remembrance and the taking of a photograph in tribute to one of the 60,000 'Diggers' who fell in action in the years 1914–1918 was a service able to be offered.

One summer evening before the sounding of Last Post at Ypres, Tony Spagnoly walked to the Belgian Battery Corner Cemetery finding this tranquil part of Flanders with not a soul about.

He located Alf Stewart's grave in this small plot sited in a side street off the main road, almost within touching distance of Ypres town's magnificent spires.

He left a poppy tribute on Alf's grave, remembered him in the register on behalf of the family and hoped the photographs he took for them would develop well (which they did).

The bells of St Martins Cathedral in Ypres gave a magnificent point to the setting, and taking another fill of the scene, a look at the grave, and a whispered "Sleep easy Alf", Tony made the journey back to Ypres.

Alf Stewart had been remembered, the search for him had come full circle. As mother church says traditionally:

'In remembrance lies immortality'

Alfred Stewart's headstone in Belgian
Battery Corner Cemetery.
Plot II. Row F. Grave 25.

Mouse Trap Farm
YPRES 11/6/25

D.H.BURLES.

D H Burles' rendering of Mouse Trap Farm, in 1925. Known by the locals before the war as Château du Nord, by British Staff as C22.b (Trench map reference). Regimental officers and troops as Shell Trap Farm (some units called it Canadian Farm) and the Germans as Wieltje Farm. Its name was later changed to Mouse Trap Farm by V Corps Command as Shell Trap Farm was considered an ill-omen and bad for troop morale. Practically all the farm names appearing on British trench maps were designated during and after the April-May 1915 battles and were not featured on existing maps at the time.

*And where the earth was soft for flowers*
*we made a grave for him that he might better rest*
'A Soldier's Grave' Francis Ledwidge




10

A BROTHERLY LOVE
Three McDonnell Brothers
2nd Battalion Royal Dublin Fusiliers, Ypres, April–May 1915.

I T WAS THE SIGHT OF ONE particular wreath set aside from the many
placed after the evening sounding of Last Post at the Menin Gate,
Ypres, that enduring tribute by the people of Ypres to the fallen of
the British and Empire army of 1914-1918, which caught the
attention as the crowd dispersed one evening. It stood seemingly
remote from the cluster placed there in the swirling wind, proclaiming:

> May the Lord have mercy on their souls
> Ar Dheis Dia go Rhaibh a Anam
> *(May their souls be on the right side of God)*
> Ireland will never forget them.

The wreath was the annual tribute by the Royal Dublin Fusiliers
Association, and recalled proudly the memory of the three McDonnell
brothers who served together with the 2nd Battalion, and fell in the
vicinity of this famous old town as the Second Ypres battles of 1915
raging to it's northeast came to a bruising finish. Reading the emotive
words and wondering who they were, set off a desire to determine how
destiny had caught up with three Irish brothers seemingly linked in
this most poignant fashion.

In the spring of 1915, the quiet streets of Dublin were awash with
grief as the casualty lists of the two battalions of the Royal Dublin
Fusiliers became known, with resounding shock and horror.

Away in far off Gallipoli taking part in that ill-fated expedition, the
1st Battalion, 'Neill's Blue Caps', serving with the 86th Brigade, 29th
Division had incurred a total loss of 700 men. Nearer home in
Flanders, as the overstretched British Forces heroically kept the
enemy from the gates of Ypres, the 2nd Battalion, part of 10th Infantry
Brigade, 4th Division, had been rushed up from the Ploegsteert area to
help plug the gap along the pitiless plain which swept around the
smallish village of St. Julien sitting astride the main
Ypres–Polecappelle road running northeast out of the town of Ypres.
Here, the 2nd Battalion played its part gallantly in keeping the

Germans at bay after their initial successes with the first gas attacks on 22 April 1915 which nearly broke the Allied line. The Dubliners lost a further 600 men bringing further pain to those they had left behind in Ireland.

The British line, though close to breaking and dangerously thin at times, never broke and their endurance and determination paid off when the German Command, unable to accommodate the savage losses being sustained, called off the battle in late May after losing 34,000 men killed, wounded and missing. The Dubliners had been heavily involved in the close combat fighting around Shell Trap Farm and the Mauser Ridge where their dogged tenacity had been vital. Losses had been heavy and when the Germans stepped back a little to get some air, the three McDonnell brothers who had fought shoulder to shoulder in the 2nd Battalion, had fallen, Peter on the 26 April and the younger Patrick and John on 24 May. In the ferocity of the fighting which marked this battle, no graves were ever found to mark their remains, and their names are commemorated for evermore on the panels of the Menin Gate at Ypres.

Over 200,000 men from the southern states in Ireland had volunteered to enlist with the British, and nearly 25,000 fell in the conflict. Men like the poet, Francis Ledwidge, 1st Battalion Royal Inniskilling Fusiliers, who was killed in 1917 near Boesinghe and buried in Artillery Wood Cemetery, and William Redmond MP, 6th Battalion, Royal Irish Regiment who died of shock at the Hospice in Locre in 1917 having been wounded near Wyteschaete and now lying alongside the military cemetery near by the Hospice, Both must have wondered how they had contrived to serve in the uniform of what many viewed as an occupying power at the time, but as Ledwidge said when volunteering in 1914:

> With the better question of Home Rule for Ireland in the balance, the aim of the volunteers was to receive and maintain the rights and liberties common to the whole people of Ireland.

It is not known what political thoughts might have impelled the McDonnell brothers to march off to war together, but there would have been no doubt of the pride, viewed with trepidation, of Mrs Anne and Mr Edmund McDonnell as they saw their sons walk away down Bride Street, Dublin; away into history. Peter was the oldest at 42, followed by Patrick, 32, and then John, at 22. It seems from their regimental numbers that they were professional soldiers, although Peter, the oldest, was probably a reservist recalled to the colours. The parents might have felt some sort of ease that the two younger sons, even though grown men, would be under the watchful eye of the eldest,

Peter, as they all entered the harsh discipline of military life together.

Families all over the United Kingdom were being shattered by the news of the loss of loved ones over the war years, but the hurt and shock Mrs McDonnell would feel on receiving the news of the deaths of her three sons can only be imagined.

To briefly trace the course of battle in April–May 1915 in front of St Julien and the Steenbeke River is not easy as Second Ypres at this stage was a maelstrom of action.

On 24 April the Dubliners took up positions in the Wieltje–St Julien line near Van Heule Farm a quarter of a mile from and facing St Julien itself. They suffered intense shelling throughout the 24th and 25th and, at dawn on the 26th a robust British counter-attack in the area helped steady the line which had begun to wilt under the enemy gas onslaught of two days before. Although not involved in the attack, the battalion experienced extreme bouts of artillery shelling, taking toll of its numbers throughout the day. Peter McDonnell, the eldest of the brothers fell on this day. So much for the fervent hope of his mother that he would be there to look after the younger two. She would not know of Peter's death in action until later in the year. If he received a soldier's grave on the meadows before St. Julien it would have been lost in the ensuing shelling. His commanding officer, Lieut.-Col.

Van Heule Farm today, still sitting alongside the Wieltje–St Julien road.

Loveband, always recognisable by his old British 'Warm' overcoat and stout blackthorn stick, was wounded in this action. Although handing over command on the day, he was soon to recover only to be killed in the same area one month later. He is commemorated on the Menin Gate at Ypres.

Fate was conspiring that Patrick and John would not be long in following their older sibling to an honourable death in action.

The battalion remained in their trenches through the rest of April and were relieved on 5 May to rest in bivouacs at Château de Trois Tours on the west bank of the Canal de L'Yser. On the 8th, the battalion marched through La Brique and St. Jean to take up positions in the woods near Potijze Château. From here they deployed for attack three times on a line between the Château and Wieltje only to have it cancelled three times due to heavy and accurate German machine-gun fire which did considerable damage to the battalion's strength. On 9 May it moved to trenches in the GHQ Line where it suffered, to quote the battalion war diary: "One of the worst day's shelling the battalion was to experience". This together with incessant sniping on the part of the enemy caused casualties the battalion could ill afford. Intermittent shelling took further casualties for the next three days before relief saw the battalion march back through St. Jean and

Mouse Trap Farm today, rebuilt after the war approximately 200 yards south of its original site which still contains remnants of its original moat.

# A BROTHERLY LOVE

Ypres on the evening of the 12th for a much needed rest in bivouacs in the grounds of Vlamertinghe Château. On 16 May it was on the march again, this time to trenches in the Divisional Support Line with its HQ in Wieltje Farm. Two days later the battalion moved into the front line trenches running from Shell Trap Farm to a point 100 yards, west of the Wieltje–St Julien road. For the next four days they were under frequent bombardment and ever present sniping. During this period, at 4 pm on the 22nd and 5.30 pm on the 23rd, it was noted that an enemy aircraft swooped low over Shell Trap Farm. Col. Loveband rightly suspected a pending attack. To quote a report on the action of 24 May by Capt. T V Linky, 2nd Royal Dublin Fusiliers;

Col. Loveband, Major Magan (2nd in C), Russell (R.A.M.C) and I (A/Adj) had just finished dinner in our H.Qr. dug outs (C.22 central) at 2:30 a.m. Previous to this the Col. and Magan had been all round the front line trenches and spent considerable time in SHELL TRAP FARM. Something suggested "gas" to the Col. during his round of the trenches as he personally warned all coy. officers to be prepared and Russell had inspected all the Vermoral sprayers and warned each company about damping their respirators. There were ten (10) sprayers in working order that night – one with each M.G. and remainder distributed along the trenches.

At 2.45 am on 24 May a red light was seen thrown up by the Germans northwest of Shell Trap Farm followed by three more directly over the farm, then a few more to the southeast of the Dubliners' trenches. Then, to quote again from Capt. Linky's report:

A few seconds later a dull roar was heard more of an explosion (certainly not a shell) and we saw the gas coming on either side of Shell Trap Farm. The Col. shouted "Get your respirators boys, here comes the gas". We had only just time to get our respirators on before the gas was over us – the Doctor (Russell) who was seeing to other people got some gas before his own respirator was adjusted.

Fortunately for the troops in the trenches 'Stand To' was just over and rum was being issued, so every one was awake and, other than the element of surprise at seeing the gas, they were soon prepared for it. There was a gentle breeze and the gas came drifting down wind toward the British line in a solid bank some 3 miles in length and 40 feet deep. There was a gentle breeze, the gas was very dense and it took some time to pass over. All signs of nature were enveloped and obliterated by this rolling cloud of agonising death, the grass was bleached and the trees left leafless, leaving behind a broad scar of destruction. The gas took about three-quarters-of-an hour to clear but, because of the early preparation by the Dublin's troops, did not cause as much damage to them as would have been expected. The real

125

danger came immediately following the gas. German infantry in small numbers moved forward rapidly occupying Shell Trap Farm and entering and holding nearby trenches as men were leaving them. Then, again in small numbers and under cover of enfilade fire, they continued this tactic, eventually taking full occupation of the farm and the trenches to the left of it. Then, supported by heavy artillery and gas shelling targeting the second and support trenches of the 2nd Battalion, they started to move into and occupy the trenches to the right of the farm, now . Enfilade fire, particularly that of machine-guns was making the Dubliners position untenable and then Col. Loveband was hit from behind with a bullet passing straight through the heart. He died without a word. All but one of the officers were now dead or wounded and the situation was desperate. By 2.30 pm the enemy was in full occupation of the battalion's front line trenches. Enemy shelling ceased but his machine-gun and rifle fire increased, the machine-gunners and infantry targeting anything that moved in their sights until dusk when, with the help of darkness, the remnants of the 2nd Battalion Dublin Fusiliers moved out of the line at 9.30 pm to bivouacs on the west bank of the canal one-and-half miles from La Brique.

Toward the end of his report Capt. Linky records:

When the wounded were sent away after dark there were no Dublins in front of Battn. H.Qrs. from about 2:30 p.m. there was no fighting in our trenches. Everyone held on to them to the last. There was no surrender, no retirement and no quarter was given or accepted. They all died fighting in their posts.

At 9:30 p.m. I received the following message:– "Please withdraw your H.Qrs. and and all men in the Retrenchment if any are still there, and report at Bde. H.Qrs. west of Canal".

The battalion strength at the start of the action on the morning of 24 May 1915 was 17 officers and 651 other ranks. At the withdrawal late that evening, mustered only one officer and 20 other ranks.

Both John and Patrick McDonnell fell this day, They together with 143 others from the 2nd Dublin Fusiliers who fell on that momentous day at St. Julien, have no known graves, and are remembered on the Menin Gate at Ypres. Most of the other ranks who fell were Reservists and Reinforcement drafted in as replacements to make up the casualties of 15 officers and 495 other ranks from the 25 April attack.

A day or two later the enemy called off his relentless pressure. 34,000 casualties was too heavy a bill for him to pay, and the determined defence of the British and Irish around Shell Trap Farm and Mauser Ridge had denied him his breakthrough.

The brothers Peter, John and Patrick McDonnell are no more, but live in memory – their names carved in stone on the Menin Gate and by the wreath left annually by the Royal Dublin Fusiliers Association. They are not forgotten even though their soldiers' graves cannot be visited, or photographs of them left to look at. Tribute can be paid though by standing south of St Julien near Van Heule Farm and gazing across to the old battleground beyond Mouse Trap Ridge. Their remains still possibly lie in those quiet pastures, together with those of their comrades. Three brothers who 'went a soldiering' together, and are now at peace, bonded in that most poignant brotherhood of all.

Recalling the memory of the McDonnell brothers brings back the shattering events that took place around Ypres in the spring period of 1915, and particularly in the area of the St. Julian road near Van Heule Farm. In a westerly direction toward Mouse Trap Ridge a thin line of defenders held off overwhelming enemy forces, obstructing their move towards the gates of Ypres. Suffering clouds of choking gas and ferocious infantry attacks while under relentless and devastating artillery bombardment, the line held until an exasperated enemy, realising the futility of his tactics, and suffering horrific losses himself, broke off his action and called it a day.

Looking across to the ridge today toward the much bigger and more industrious farm complex of buildings once known to British troops as Shell Trap, and then Mouse Trap farm, the visitor is looking across the slopes that were once an area of heroic defence and sacrifice, with the efforts of the Irish regiments in particular being nothing short of epic. Within the sweep of the eye, beneath that peaceful landscape, lie the earthly remains of a long catalogue of Irishmen whose names alone are recorded on the Menin Gate memorial at Ypres. The McDonnells with many of their fellow Dubliners lie there. There are no graves to visit, but this ridge is a much a part of Ireland as it is of Belgium.

Poor Mrs McDonnell may not have had a chance to mourn for her lost sons all those years ago, but it can be done on her behalf by those who pass this way on the on the road to St Julien.

Her sons were at least saved the disappointment that ripped apart the loyal military traditions of five proud Irish regiments in the post war years when the government of the time decided that Ireland's best, amongst other regiments of the line, should be disbanded and obliged to hand over their colours. Sir L. Worthington Evans, then Secretary of State for War, published a statement to the effect that:

In order to effect the necessary economy demanded by the finances of the country, it has been decided to reduce the Regular Army by 5 line cavalry regiments, or an equivalent reduction, and 24 line battalions and corresponding depots.

Handing over the colours to His Majesty the King, St Georges Hall, Windsor Castle, 12 June 1922

The resulting Army Order No. 78, as far as the infantry of the Army was concerned, was published on 11 March 1922. At the time the 2nd Battalion Royal Dublin Fusiliers were in India, returning from there to join the 1st Battalion at Bordon barracks on 28 April where both battalions began the heart-breaking processes of disbandment.

On 12 June, the Colours were handed over to the British King in St. Georges Hall, Windsor Castle. At the end of the ceremony the King handed each of the colonels a letter of goodbye addressed to each regiment, recalling its past history and expressing his grateful thanks and appreciation of services rendered. Of the 1st and 2nd Battalions Dublin Fusiliers he was to say in the letter:

It is with feelings of no ordinary sorrow that I address you for the last time, for I know that I am taking leave, not merely of a fine Regiment, but of great memories and great traditions which hitherto have been kept alive and embodied in you.

You are the oldest of the British garrison in India. Your Second Battalion dates back to the time when Queen Catherine of Braganza brought Bombay as part of her dowry to King Charles II; your First Battalion to still remoter days. Stringer Lawrence, the teacher of Robert Clive, won many a victory with you. Clive led you to Arcot and Plassey; Eyre Coote to Wandewash; Forde to Condore.

Your history is the early history of British dominance in India, and you have shown abundantly that you could fight as sternly in South Africa and in Europe as in the East Indies.

To me it is a mournful task to bid you farewell. I have always taken the greatest pride in your past history, but if the glory of any fighting men be safe, then most assuredly safe is yours....

Peter, John and Patrick McDonnell would have been proud of that.

Elverdinghe church in the early post war years.

*I salute the Glorious Dead*
*who did not live to see the success of their endeavour.*
Roger Keyes

11
OUT ELVERDINGHE WAY
With an artist in the Salient.

THERE WAS ONLY one way to describe it: "It was a golden morning", simply perfect, with the Flemish sunlight shining on the countryside and bringing out all the colours that would have delighted the Flemish painting school several centuries back. The offer of a drive to Elverdinghe northwest of Ypres with an artist friend who wished to put 'brush to palette' and 'to capture the moment' as he put it, I found hard to resist. I was quite happy to go along and smell the flowers along the way.

We were in Ypres, We were there to wander the old battlefields and visit sights of the Great War. We had all the time in the world. We were in that mood – and the sun was warm on our backs as we headed out of Ypres, heading northwest to Elverdinghe.

On a quiet, dusty side road close to that village, on the road to Poperinghe, my friend the artist busied himself, sketching and painting a small red-roofed farm which had attracted his attention across the meadow, whilst from the imposing church tower at Elverdinghe peeping above a cluster of tall trees, could be heard the noonday bell. I watched him apply himself to the scene he wanted to capture before this beautiful Flemish light changed. It seemed to me a complete paradox as my mind slipped back to the war years and what had occurred locally.

After consulting maps of the of back areas, I was able to announce that, probably for the first time in its long history, Welsh Farm, both its name and long history possibly unknown to its farmer, was about to be captured on canvas for posterity. The close proximity of this rural backwater to a dozen tall plane trees, gave it, from a distance, an almost 'Corot' appearance. The famous French impressionist himself would have been proud to exploit the scene before us. Was it any wonder that, using this rather unique quality of Flemish light, an early school of impressionist painting had existed in the nearby hill town of Cassel almost one hundred years before?

131

Elverdinghe church today.

At least this would give the artist an accurate caption to apply to his work. Gazing at it through a long English winter evening before the fire, he would be reminded of a certain lovely summer day in Flanders, and also spare a thought perhaps for the many tough Welshmen who had inhabited the farm and its surrounds in July, 1917, before the 38th Welsh Division had moved up to the Pilckem Ridge via the canal crossing at Boesinghe to play their part in the Third Ypres battles. Many of these did not survive the roar and terror of battle, whilst others came back this way to have their wounds and fearful pain eased here at a First Aid Station set up at the farm. It was the thought of the spirits of those who died here that had to be addressed across these lovely meadows and to the lofty spire of Elverdinghe beyond. No cemeteries exist to ennoble the site. Perhaps the farm was considered too insignificant for such a purpose and records were not kept of the fallen here, even though the army mapmakers felt it important enough to be identified alongside the light gauge railway terminating at Elverdinghe Château, an important place at the time and the site of several senior headquarter bases. The two nearest British Military Cemeteries are to be found at Hospital Farm and Hagle Dump.

As the day wore on, we packed the paint and palette and drove round the next bend and through the silent streets of Elverdinghe.

Welsh Farm as it is today, with no cemetery or signs of the old light gauge railway to give it credence as a place of importance in the Great War.

Photograph by Sue and John Allen

Elverdinghe with its silent streets.

One of the fascinating aspects of French and Flemish villages around the lunchtime period is that they are usually devoid of all humanity. Much too civilised to rush and tear around like their Anglo-Saxon neighbours, it bears testimony to their being with the family behind the shuttered windows enjoying 'déjeuner avec la famille'. No one sallies abroad, and for once here, at least daily for an hour or two 'King Motor Car' takes a back seat.

Tranquil and deserted, except for a languid cat stretching itself in the gathering heat, the village presented itself as a picture of peace. 'A haven from hell', if only for a few grateful days, is how it must have seemed to the young men from another age who once filled these silent streets to regenerate shattered spirits with only the ever-present boom of cannon to the east for company. I tried to imagine all this through shaded lids in the heat. Men clad in khaki, free from the sight of death and destruction, with a cooling drink of cheap beer or a hastily prepared meal of 'oeufs et frites' and coffee, a luxury they had possibly looked forward to for days. It is a matter of record that many young Guardsman or Welshman enjoyed such a break before being instructed that duty called, then, buckling up heavy loads of equipment, collecting rifles, lighting up, and marching off eastward to Boesinghe and the front line of 31 July 1917 – and on into history! Many, of course, were destined never to return; but one can still feel their very presence in these quiet streets. Strangely enough, my spirit seemed troubled somewhat by this very thought. Much of the older part of Elverdinghe must be unchanged from those troubled far off days, but now parts of the village are filled with smart new villas, with the mandatory clipped lawn, and the shiny car in the driveway – a modern breed of affluent young Belgians and their families being the proud owners. The spirits of any young soldiers who wander these places can stop and ponder, satisfied that this is their legacy, that their sacrifice had brought and preserved this modern prosperity. The thought pacified me and allowed me to continue, although in a thoughtful manner. That is the sobering effect of modern Flanders.

Time to move on as the weathered stone and imposing presence of Elverdinghe Château came into view, and one could not help admiring the manicured grounds and the well cared for foliage which gave it a timeless charm. Out of range of most of the enemy guns except by the largest calibre at the latter stage of the war, the château survived the war without serious damage, even though the enemy must have known that several divisions used it for headquarters of various units, particularly leading up to the 1917 Passchendaele offensive. The Guards and the 38th Welsh Division were certainly here. The buildings were also used for several court martials, although any resulting executions were carried out nearer Poperinghe to the west. The château also came into brief prominence in a second war, 22 years later. In those dark days of 1940, during the British retreat to the beaches of the Dunkirk perimeter, a young commander of the British 3rd Division used it for his battle headquarters after a skillful defence of the canal system around Ypres which gained valuable time for the retreating troops. Major-General Bernard Law Montgomery knew it well.

Elverdinghe Château, as imposing and undamaged today as it was during the years of the Great War.

The area around Elverdinghe was well known during the Great War because of the various unit headquarters to be found here. It was also a locality populated by army camps and hospital facilities for much of the war, being out of range of enemy shellfire - even though itself a target for enemy bombers when the conditions were favourable. Rest and traing camps with names such as Dirty Bucket Camp, Welsh Camp, White Mill Camp, Bridge Camp, and the like found a prominence together with the dressing stations and hospitals clustered around the village of Brandhoek on the main Ypres to Poperinghe road. Hospital Farm[1], as the name implies, was one such place, and though remote, it is a charming place to visit and revive memories from yesteryear.

While sketching materials and creative talent again captured the scene which had suddenly presented itself, I wandered off to the military cemetery behind the farm to enjoy probably the most memorable moment in what had been a blissful day. Entering the area through its rusty turnstile gate, memories flooded back from an earlier occasion. The farm buildings were as I remembered them. Once used as a dressing station staffed by British medics, the complex was now a working Flemish farm with the odd farm animal making its presence known. In those far off days of war, the British army's light gauge railways networked the back areas, feeding this district from the direction of Poperinghe, then eastwards towards the line at Boesinghe. It no doubt brought a

Hospital Farm was used as a hospital from 1915-17. It's proximity to the front line and light gauge railways placed is ideally for housing casualties from the Salient.

regular input of suffering humanity to the farm to be assisted and attended to medically. Again, not another human or motorcar being in sight to shatter the peace of a lovely afternoon.

The magic of silence worked again. A pond lay close by, and it did not take a quantum leap of the imagination to see a group of men in hospital colours grouped around this piece of now stagnant water, chatting and taking what ease was offered, even though they were well within hearing distance of the sounds of war. The outbuilding and the farm itself itself must have been a hive of motorised activity both day and night.

A long line of stately poplars stood like sentinels between the turnstile and the little burial plot tucked away at the far end of the area. The poplars seemed to whisper together in some sort of unity and it was altogether a very special moment as I slipped into a reflective world of my own. I was forcibly reminded of a snatch of poetry about Ypres which had always inspired me; by J. L. Crommelin-Brown, who had served here with the heavy guns of the Garrison Artillery:

> Besides the road that leads to Ypres,
> They found the long roads end.
> The poplars whisper overhead,
> And still they wait those gallant dead,
> To march a mile besides a friend,
> Along the road to Ypres.

Hospital Farm Military Cemetery seen across and alongside its now stagnant pond where once men in hospital blue would gather.

That little snippet seemed to say it all at that particular moment - the sight and sounds of this lonely place!

The cemetery itself, small and typical of the area, has 115 graves - all British, The number of gunners reflect the many artillery gun-sites in the area during the war years. By the entrance is the last resting place of Special Reserve officer, Lieut. Alfred E. Voysey, aged 32, from Eastbourne, Sussex. During the intensive enemy counter barrages in the days leading up to the opening of Third Ypres, he had been badly wounded near Boesinghe on 29 July 1917 while seconded to the Royal Garrison Artillery (attached to 21st Heavy Battery), He had succumbed to his wounds at Hospital Farm and was buried here with those whispering poplars for company.

The son of a clergyman, the family wording engraved on his head stone seems to epitomise this fact:

*When Christ appears, then shall he also appear with him - in glory*

Also buried in this small cemetery is a young Royal Dublin Fusilier who was killed in action on 8 July 1915 in the aftermath of the Second Ypres actions. Private Michael Condon, 19-year old lad from Waterford, brings to mind that other young soldier buried close by at Poelcappelle: John Condon, Royal Irish Rifles, aged 14, allegedly the youngest soldier to fall, who also hailed from the Emerald Isle. Could they have been related? No reasons are given why a Belgian or French civilian lies in this plot. Could Marcel Top have been a civilian working for the army and caught up in the general mayhem of the regular air raids that shattered this area?

Now they are all linked in that brotherhood of eternal rest.

A light hoot of the car's horn brought me back to my senses. On then to Hagle Dump Cemetery, turning left at Dirty Bucket Corner[2] then down the long winding road to this quiet, isolated little cemetery. Hagle Dump has always fascinated me. Who or what was Hagle? The cemetery itself lends more to the 1918 Battle of Lys period and the plot was developed as the larger nearby Hospital Farm became full. It transpires that Hagle was the name of a Pioneer officer whose name was given, either by him, his senior officer or his men, to a small salvage dump he sited in this area. Very few of the almost 500 British Military Cemeteries in Belgium are identified with a personal name. Pioneer Officer Hagle might well have been proud to know that one of them would be named after him and, because of that, his name will forever live in Belgian Flanders – or at least until the unthinkable happens and, for whatever reason, the British Military Cemeteries are no more. What a thought! Again the light hoot of the car's horn brought me back to my sense and drove that particular one from my mind – this glorious day did not merit such thinking.

The light was beginning to go as the sun slid into the west, and we were ready to return to the hotel in Ypres.

For almost two hours, we had not seen another human being or a motor car in the peaceful back areas near Elverdinghe. Yes, these back areas offer a Flanders in its purist form: tranquil and serene; the land of poets and artists; the land of mists and mystery, and a place full of spirits from another age! Visitors will be well rewarded for the time they are able to spend here.

1. The name Hospital Farm was not given to it by the troops or military mapmakers as the cemetery register says. Although this was generally the case with English names identifying trench map references, Hospital Farm is a literal translation of the French, Hôpital Ferme, and appeared on pre-war Belgian maps in that form. It poses the question as to why a French and not Flemish name was attributed to a remote farmstead in Belgian West Flanders.

2. As with Hospital Farm, Dirty Bucket is a direct translation of the name of an estaminet that stood on this corner, which also gave its name to a railway siding, Dirty Bucket Sidings and one of many camps sited in the area, Dirty Bucket Camp.

Hagle Dump Cemetery.

# BIBLIOGRAPHY

**2nd City of London Regiment (Royal Fusiliers) in the Great War.**
By Major W E Grey. Headquarters of the Regiment. London 1929.
**A Student in Arms.** By Donald Hankey. Andrew Melrose Ltd. London 1916
**British Regiments, 1914–1918.**
By Brigadier A E James, OBE, TD. Samsons Books Ltd. London 1978.
**Chavasse Double V.C.**
By Ann Clayton. Leo Cooper, London 1992
**Essex Units in the Great War 1914-1918. 2nd Battalion Essex Regiment Vol 2.**
By John Wm Burrows FSA. John Burrows & Sons, Southend-on-Sea 1927.
**Balliol College War Memorial, Book II.**
Robert Maclehose and Co. Ltd. University Press, Glasgow 1925.
**Extracts from the Diary of a Soldier.** By A. D. Strange-Boston, C. E. ma.
**Gilbert Walter Lyttelton Talbot.** By his Mother. Printed for private circulation.
Charles Whittingham & Co. London 1916.
**History of the Great War. Military Operations, France and Belgium, 1915,
Volumes I and II.**
Compiled by Brig.-Gen. Sir James Edmonds CB, CMG, RE (Retired) psc.
Macmillan and Co. Ltd. London 1928.
**Infanterie Regiment 126 im Weltkrieg.** Germany
**Letters of Donald Hankey "A Student in Arms".**
Compiled by Edward Miller MA. Andrew Melrose Ltd. London 1919.
**Neill's "Blue Caps". Vol. III 1914–1922.**
By Colonel H C Wylly, CB. Gale & Polden Ltd. 1923.
**Orange, Green and Khaki.**
By Tom Johnstone. Gill & MacMillan, Dublin 1992.
**Pass Guard at Ypres.**
By Ronald Gurner. J M Dent & Sons Ltd. London 1930.
**Raymond Revised.** By Sir Oliver J Lodge. Psychic Book Club Ltd. London
**Rifle Brigade Chronicle 1918.** Compiled and Edited by Col. Willoughby Verner.
John Bale, Sons & Danielsson Ltd. London 1919.
**Soldiers Died in the Great War 1914–1919, Part 57 The King's Royal Rifle
Corps.** J B Hayward & Son. Suffolk 1989.
**Soldiers Died in the Great War 1914–1919, Part 74 The Rifle Brigade (The
Prince Consort's Own).** J B Hayward & Son. Suffolk 1988
**The 33rd Division in France and Flanders 1915–1919.**
By Lieutenant-Colonel Graham Seton Hutchison DSO, MC, FRGS.
Waterlow & sons Ltd. London 1921.
**The Annals of the King's Royal Rifle Corps. Volume V. The Great War.**
By Major-General Sir Stuart Hare KCMG CB.
John Murray, London 1932.
**The Battle Book of Ypres.**
Compiled by Beatrice Brice. John Murray, London 1927
**The Border Regiment in The Great War.**
By Colonel H C Wylly CB. Gale & Polden Ltd. Aldershot 1924.
**The Duke of Cornwall's Light Infantry 1914-1919.**
By Edward Wyrall. Methuen & Co. Ltd. London 1932.
**The Great War as I saw it.**
By Canon Frederick George Scott, CGM, DSO.
The Clarke and Stuart Co. Ltd. Vancouver 1934.
**The History of the King's Regiment (Liverpool) 1914-1918 Vol I.**
By Edward Wyrall. Edward Arnold & Co. London 1928.

# BIBLIOGRAPHY

**The History of the King's Shropshire Light Infantry in the Great War 1914-18.**
Edited by W de B Wood. The Medici Society Ltd. London 1925.
**The History of the Rifle Brigade in the War of 1914-1918.**
By Reginald Berkeley MC. The Rifle Brigade Club Ltd. London 1927.
**The History of the Somerset Light Infantry 1914-1919.**
By Edward Wyrall. Methuen & Co. Ltd. London 1927.
**The Immortal Salient.**
Compiled by Lieut.-Gen. Sir William Pulteney and Beatrix Brice. John Murray for The Ypres League. London 1925
**The King's Royal Rifle Corps Chronicle. 1915. 1916.**
Warren and Son Ltd. Winchester. 1916. 1919.
**The King's Royal Rifle Corps Chronicle. 1917.**
John Murray. London 1920.
**The King's Royal Rifle Corps Association Journal 2000.**
The King's Royal Rifle Corps Association. London 2000.
**The Official History of the War. Military Operations France and Belgium 1915.**
Compiled by Brig.-Gen. Sir James E Edmonds Cb, CMG, RE (Retired), psc.
MacMillan and Co. Ltd., London 1928.
**The Official History of the Canadian Army in the First World War.**
**Canadian Expeditionary Force 1914–1918.**
By Col. G W L Nicholson, C.D. Authority of the MOD. Ottawa 1962
**The OTC and the Great War.**
By Captain Alan R Haig-Brown. George Newnes Ltd. London 1915
**The Ox & Bucks Light Infantry Chronicle. 1915–1916.**
Compiled and Edited by Lieut.-Col. A F Mockler-Ferryman.
Eyre and Spottiswoode Ltd.
**The Pilgrim's Guide to the Ypres Salient.**
Herbert Reiach Ltd. for Talbot House. London 1920.
**The Silent Cities.**
Compiled by Sidney Hurst P A S I. Methuen & Co Ltd. London 1929
**The VC and DSO. Volume I.**
By Sir O'Moore Creagh VC, GCB, GCSI and E M Humphris.
The Standard Art Book Co Ltd. London 1924
**The Worcestershire Regiment in the Great War.**
By Captain H FitzM Stacke MC. GT Cheshire & Sons Ltd. Kidderminster 1918.
**War Letters of Fallen Englishmen.**
Edited by Laurence Housman. Victor Gollancz Ltd. London 1930.
**With Riflemen, Scouts and Snipers, from 1914-1919.**
By Major F M Crum King's Royal Rifle Corps.
Printed for private circulation. Oxford 1921.
**Ypres Before and After the Great War.**
Bernard S A. Liege 1919.

**Private Papers.**
Davis family compiled by Ken Davis.
Nick Fear.
Mary Ellen Freeman.
Rae family papers
Tony Spagnoly.
Ted Smith.

# INDEX

## Military Units

1/4th Royal Berks: 103, 105, 108
100th Infantry Brigade: 89
104th M. G. Coy.: 80
10th DLI: 5
10th Canadian Siege Bty: 82
10th Infantry Brigade: 123
10th King's Liverpools: 103, 107
126 Infanterie Regiment: 23, 25
14th (Light) Division: x, 2, 5, 22, 13, 35, 45, 50, 51
16th KRRC: 89
17th Battalion, A.I.F.: 111, 112, 115, 116
18th and 14th Brigades: 45
1/8th Sherwood Foresters: 33
1st Canadian Corps: 69
1st Dublin Fusiliers: 121, 129
1st Royal Inniskillings: 124
1st Gloucestershires: 30
1st Groupe Provisoire Regt D'Artillerie: 119
20th Brigade: 51
21st Heavy Battery: 140
25th Brigade: 69
27th New York Division: 79
29th Division: 123
2nd Dublins Fusiliers: 123, 127, 128, 131
2nd Worcesters: 87, 91
2nd South Lancs: 55
30th Tennessee Div.: 79
38th Welsh Division: 135, 137
3rd and 14th Divisions: 3
3rd South Lancs: 56
3rd Division: 5, 137
3rd Rifle Brigade: 41, 42, 65
41st Brigade: x, 35, 36, 38, 45, 48, 50, 51, 67, 69
42nd Brigade: 3, 36, 38, 48, 67
43rd Brigade: 3, 36, 45, 47, 48
46th Division: 45, 48

48th Midland Division: 103
49th Division: 45
4th Division: 5, 123
4th Middlesex: 32
5th Australian Division: 112
5th KSLI: 3, 5, 7
5th Ox & Bucks: 3, 5
5th Royal Berks: 17
6th DCLI: v, 1, 2, 3, 7, 11, 36, 38, 45, 47, 48
6th Royal Irish Regt.: 124
6th Div.: 42, 45, 48, 62
7th Infantry Brigade: 55
7th KRRC: 35, 36, 38, 51
7th Rifle Brigade: 32, 36, 38, 40, 42, 51, 67, 77
7th Brigade: 62, 107
7th London Brigade R.G.A.: 77
7th Royal Sussex: 17
7th, 8th and 9th Brigades: 60
86th Brigade: 123
88th Brigade: 87
8th KRRC: 17, 36, 38, 51, 67, 69
8th Rifle Brigade: 17, 29, 35, 36, 38, 39, 40, 41, 51, 77
8th Brigade: 61, 63
8th Division: 119
9th KRRC: 36, 37, 38, 45, 47, 48, 51
9th Rifle Brigade: 3, 4, 5, 8, 7, 17, 36, 37, 47
9th Brigade: 19, 103, 107
Anzac Division: 117
Artist Rifles: 87
Australian 2nd Div: 113, 116
British Second Corps: 79
Canadian Artillery: 84
Canadian Corps: 82
Canadian Field Artillery: 82
Canadian First Division: 84
Ceylon Planters Rifles: 67
Dartmouth Volunteer Training Unit: 81

French XXXVI Corps: 45
Hampshire Regiment: 105
Kitchener's New Army: 1, 5, 13, 17, 38, 67
Military Police: 9
Neill's Blue Caps': 123
No. 2 Group Heavy Artillery Reserve: 48
Officer Training Corps: 5, 13, 16, 38, 76
RFC Squadron: 45
Royal Dublin Fusiliers: 123
Royal Engineers: 45, 59
Royal Flying Corps: 10
Royal Garrison Artillery: 140
Royal Irish Rifles: 140
Royal Scots Regiment: 101
Second Army: 50
The Guards: 137
Trench Mortar Batteries: 45
VI Corps: 48, 50
Welch Regiment: 1
Worcestershire Regiment: 87

## Cemeteries

Artillery Wood Cemetery: 124
Abeele Airfield Cemetery: 80
Achiet-le-Grand Communal Cemetery Ext.: 32
Barlin Communal Cemetery Extension: 53
Bècourt Military Cemetery: 32
Belgian Battery Corner Cemetery: 119, 121
Berlin South Western Cemetery: 33
Bernafay Wood British Cemetery: 33
Birr Cross Roads Cemetery: 65
Brandhoek New Military Cemetery: 103
Delville Wood Cemetery: 65
Dozinghem Military Cemetery: 80, 85
Essex Farm Cemetery: 77
Hagle Dump Cemetery: 140, 141
Holywell Cemetery: 32, 109
Hooge Crater Cemetery: x, 44

# INDEX

# INDEX

Lawrence, Cpl. : 41
Lawrence, Stringer: 129
Ledwidge, Francis: 124
Leonard:, Mrs 64
Linky, Capt. T V: 127
Lodge, Lady Mary: 64
Lodge, Oliver and Mary: 55
Lodge, Sir Oliver: 55, 64
Lodge, 2nd-Lt. R.: 52, 55
Loveband, Lt.-Col.: 125, 127
Lyttelton, Gen. Sir Neville,
G.C.B: 18, 32
MacAfee, Lt. L. A.: 39
Maclachlan, Lt.-Col R. 16,
21, 32, 36, 51
Magan, Maj.: 127
Maj.-Gen. Commanding
36th (Ulster) Division: 51
Marion, Tom: 116
Maxwell, Lieut.-Col. J. M.C.
D.S.O.: 65, 66, 67, 73
Maxwell, Maj. J: 69, 74, 76
McAlpine, Mr Bob: 121
McDonnell, John and
Patrick: 126
McDonnell, Mrs Anne and
Mr Edmund: 124
McDonnell, Peter, John and
Patrick: 125, 129, 131
Merrill, Samuel and Estelle
Hatch: 80
Merrill, Wainwright: 79, 82,
83, 84
Milsom, 2nd-Lt.: 26, 27, 29,
31, 33
Montgomery, Maj.-Gen.
Bernard Law: 137
Myers: 64, 65
Nash, Rfn. G. H.: 42, 51
Newbolt, Sir Henry: 101
Nugent, Brig.-Gen. O., DSO,
ADC: 39, 45, 49, 51
Osler, 2nd-Lt. Revere: 80,
85
Pawle, Capt.: 19, 26, 27, 33,
31
Plumer, Gen.: 63
Pointon, 2nd-Lt.: 95
Poulton, Mr: 22
Poulton, 2nd-Lt. R: 14, 15,
17, 18, 22, 32, 101, 102,
103, 105, 107, 109
Rae, Edward: 13, 33

Rae, Lieut, K: 13, 14, 19,
27, 29
Rae, Margaret: 33
Raymond, Pte.: 57
Redmond, William, MP:
124
Reiss, 2nd-Lt. S.: 15, 17,
32
Rennie, Lt.-Col. G.AP,
DSO: 51
Rittsen-Thomas, Lt.: 65
Revere, Paul: 80
Rogers, Rfn. H.: 29, 33
Roscoe, Lt. W.: 55, 61, 63
Russell (R.A.M.C): 127
Salter, Capt. Reginald: 60,
65
Saxby, Cpl.: 33
Scott, Sir Walter: 77
Scrimgeour: 20
Sheepshanks, Capt. A. C.:
20, 33, 36, 51
Skinner, Brig.-Gen. P. B.
C., CMG, DSO: 71, 72, 75
Smith, F. E.: 15
Stanley, A. A.: 79
Stewart, L/Cpl., Alfr: 111,
112, 117, 118, 120, 121
Stokoe, Col. T. R.: 4, 9
Stoney, Lt.-Col.: 91, 92, 95
Strange Boston, Rfn.: 39
Talbot, Edward, Bishop of
Winchester: 32
Talbot, Lt.: 32, 42, 51
Talbot, Neville: 42, 43, 14,
32
Taylor, Capt.: 63
Templar, Capt. Claude: 3
Thomas, Charles: 57, 61
Tillet Rfn.: 32
Top, Marcel: 139
Turner, Lt. F. H.: 101, 102,
103, 107, 108, 109
Ventris, 2nd-Lt.: 63, 65
Voysey, Lt. Alfred E: 140
Wace, Capt. P.: 16, 17, 32
Wall, Maj. A. H.: 16
Washington, George: 80
Watson, Sgt.: 118
Wollinsky, Lt. A.: 13, 24,
26, 33
Woodroffe, Capt. L.: 17, 27,
40, 51

Woodroffe, 2nd-Lt. S. C.:
17, 19, 22, 29, 32, 33, 41,
42, 44, 51
Woods, 2nd-Lt. R. H.: 69
Lawrence, Stringer: 133
Wynne-Wilson, Rev. St. J.
B.: 16

**British Trenches/
Strongpoints**
Anton's Farm: 105, 107
Anzac: 116, 117
Army Line: 89, 92, 93
Bond Street: 47
C.22 central: 120, 125
Divisional Support line:
127
Fleet Street: 44, 47
GHQ line: 7, 60, 126
Loos–Givenchy line: 2
Munster Alley: 113
New Bond Street: xi, 44
Old Bond Street: xi, 44, 46
Shrapnel Gulley: 116
The Culvert: x, 36, 37, 44,
47, 48
The Stables: x, 44, 62, 65
The Strand: 44, 47, 114
Trench G10: 23, 33
Trench G3: 33
Trench G5: 23, 24, 26, 29,
30, 33, 62, 63, 65
Wieltje–St Julien line: 125
Y Sap: 113

**Rest & Training Camps**
Aldershot Camp: 67, 71
B Camp: 69
Bridge Camp: 138
Bristol Castle: 67
Bullring: 115
California Camp: 69
Chippewa Camp: 67
Dirty Bucket Camp: 138,
141
Ridge Wood: 59,67
Welsh Camp: 138
White Mill Camp: 138
Valcartier Camp: 82

144

# INDEX

# INDEX